Jacob of Sarug's Homily on Zacchaeus the Tax Collector

Texts from Christian Late Antiquity

6

Series Editor
George Anton Kiraz

TeCLA (Texts from Christian Late Antiquity) is a new series presenting ancient Christian texts both in their original languages and with accompanying contemporary English translations.

Jacob of Sarug's Homily on Zacchaeus the Tax Collector

Metrical Homilies of Mar Jacob of Sarug

Fascicle 30

Translated by

Dana Miller

Edited with Notes and Introduction by
Mary T. Hansbury

gorgias press
2010

Gorgias Press LLC, 954 River Road, Piscataway, NJ, 08854, USA

www.gorgiaspress.com

Copyright © 2010 by Gorgias Press LLC

All rights reserved under International and Pan-American Copyright Conventions. No part of this publication may be reproduced, stored in a retrieval system or transmitted in any form or by any means, electronic, mechanical, photocopying, recording, scanning or otherwise without the prior written permission of Gorgias Press LLC.

2010   ܟܒ

ISBN 978-1-61719-660-7   ISSN 1935-6846

Library of Congress Cataloging-in-Publication Data
Jacob, of Serug, 451-521.
  [Homily on Zacchaeus the tax collector. English & Syriac]
  Jacob of Sarug's Homily on Zacchaeus the tax collector / translated by Dana Miller, Mary Hansbury.
       p. cm. -- (Texts from Christian late antiquity ; 6) (Metrical homilies of Mar Jacob of Sarug)
  Includes bibliographical references and index.
 1. Zacchaeus (Biblical figure)--Sermons. 2. Sermons, Syriac. 3. Sermons, Syriac--Translations into English. I. Miller, Dana. II. Hansbury, Mary. III. Title.
  BS2520.Z3J33 2010
  226.4'06--dc22

2010050017

Printed in the United States of America

TABLE OF CONTENTS

Table of Contents v
List of Abbreviations vii
Introduction 1
    Contents 1
    The Manuscript Tradition 3
    Summary 3
Text and Translation 5
    The Path of Christ's Mercy to Heal the World 6
    Power of Repentance Reflected in Zacchaeus as in a Mirror 10
    The Light of Grace Dawns in Zacchaeus' Soul 16
    Zacchaeus Climbs Up to Gaze and the Sight of the Lord Fashions
        Him Anew 22
    The Gaze of Zacchaeus at Christ Is Transformed by Christ's Love .. 26
    Christ the Husbandman, by His Teaching Redeems the World 30
    Zacchaeus as a First Fruit among Sinners 36
    The Lord of the World Reclines in the House of Zacchaeus 42
    At the Great Banquet, Yoked by Christ, Zacchaeus Begins to
        Lavish his Wealth upon the Needy 46
    A Soul Restored from Wickedness is a Greater Sign than a Body's
        Resurrection from Destruction 50
Bibliography of Works Cited 57
    (A) Ancient Authors and Translations 57
    Aphrahat: 57
    Cyrillona: 57
    Ephrem: 57
    Jacob: 57
    Narsai: 58
    Odes of Solomon: 58
    Rabbinics: 58
    Theodore of Mopsuestia: 58
    (B) Modern Works 58

Index of Names and Themes 61
Index of Biblical References 63

List of Abbreviations

CD	Commentary on the Diatessaron.
CSCO	Corpus Scriptorum Christianorum Orientalium (Louvain).
ETL	*Ephemerides Theologicae Lovanienses* (Louvain).
HTR	*Harvard Theological Review* (Cambridge Mass.).
JCSSS	*Journal of the Canadian Society for Syriac Studies* (Toronto).
JNSL	*Journal of Northwest Semitic Languages* (Stellenbosch).
JTS	*Journal of Theological Studies* (Oxford).
LM	*Le Muséon* (Louvain la Neuve).
PdO	*Parole de l'Orient* (Kaslik, Lebanon).
SJT	*Scottish Journal of Theology* (Edinburgh).
Sob/ECR	*Sobornost* incorporating *Eastern Churches Review* (London).
SP	*Studia Patristica* (Louvain).
SVTQ	*St. Vladimir's Theological Quarterly* (New York).
RTP	*Revue de Théologie et de Philosophie* (Louvain/Lausanne).

INTRODUCTION

> INFORMATION ON THIS HOMILY
> Homily Title: Zacchaeus the Tax-Collector
> Source of Text: *Homiliae selectae Mar-Jacobi Sarugensis* edited by Paul Bedjan (Paris—Leipzig 1905, 2nd ed. Piscataway: Gorgias Press, 2006), vol. 1, pp. 344–64. [Homily 15]
> Lines: 400

This is the story of Zacchaeus the chief tax-collector of Jericho (Lk 9:1-10), found only in the Gospel of Luke. We are that told he was very wealthy. Yet while being a rich man, Zacchaeus provides a contrast to that other rich man in Luke's Gospel (18:18-33) who couldn't detach himself from his material possessions to follow Christ. In this verse homily/mimro, Jacob outlines how the transformation occurred in Zacchaeus.

CONTENTS

Jacob begins and ends this homily with a reference to salvation history. His Soteriology indicates not so much divine providence from the time of creation but the path (*ûrḥâ*) of Christ in the world and actually continued by the Church at His Resurrection. Christ's way is described here as He passes by those in need of repentance, those stricken with disease, sinners, the broken hearted, all awaiting the medicine of life. Only these know their need of the Physician, as did Zacchaeus seemingly intuitively. And it is the will of the Father that they be restored to the Kingdom, so Jesus goes along his way which is the will of the Father. This path (*ûrḥâ*) itself is the will of the Father (1–32).

The Saviour proceeds along his way caring specifically for Zacchaeus, leading him to repentance by healing him. Perhaps Jacob shares Ephrem's understanding of healing as a new creation. Then Christ places Zacchaeus as a mirror (*maḥzitâ*) or sign, set up along the way for all humanity to see. The very gravity of Zacchaeus's faults as a greedy extortioner, becomes a stimulus to his own conversion and only adds to the symbolic import of the conversion for all humanity (33–72).

Having heard that Jesus was passing by, Zacchaeus goes out to meet Him. As a tax-collector his vices were manifestly wicked like those of the harlot, and he carried this sickness to Jesus to be healed. It was by grace (*taybûtâ*) that this awareness developed in him. Jacob gives no other reason for his recognizing in Jesus a refuge. Then inspite of being a little man, his love and faith were so great that his mind reached heavenward. And his body reached out to the barren fig (*têtâ*), a tree with its own long history (Gen. 3:7), so as to add to his stature (73–126).

Impelled by his love Zacchaeus climbs the tree, his faith giving him new height. Immediately as he looked on Jesus he became righteous, as did the Jews who looked at the bronze serpent in the desert. Here Jacob's typology may reflect the exegesis of Theodore of Mopsuestia. Then the venom of the fiery serpent (Num. 21:6) vanishes from Zacchaeus's members. And even from a distance this transformation occurs, since nothing can keep desire (*regtâ*) from intermingling *(hûltânâ)*. Because he gazed on Christ Zacchaeus was united with Him, such is the power of love (127–166). Brought near to Christ by His love and inspite of the crowd of people Zacchaeus, recognizes Him and so begins the process of repentance, making of Zacchaeus a paradigm of salvation for "peoples, worlds and regions," much as had occurred for the Sinful Woman. It is as if love is the mediary (*meṣ'âyâ*) setting this process in motion, reflecting prevenient divine love and also the human love in response to divine love. Whereas according to Ephrem, faith is the key to understanding God's providence, for Jacob the emphasis seems to be on love, even for the understanding of Scripture. (167–202).

With the use of the term Husbandman as a Christological title and the "irrigation" of His teaching, Jacob here shows how Christ produces and receives fruit throughout the world, from a harlot, from a tax-collector, even from the stones. And now from the "desolate city" of Jericho and a barren fig tree, a cherished cluster of repentance is brought forth in Zacchaeus, even finer than the fruit in Eden (203–240). Jesus continues on his path (*ûrḥâ*), trapping Zacchaeus into repentance and making of him a pattern (*nišâ*) for others. Then Zacchaeus who is accustomed to robbing, lays hold of grace and plunders forgiveness. It comes full circle and Zacchaeus distributes his possessions, lavishing them on the poor. He stole in abundance and gave back in abundance. Here again love is the mediating force: the love of Zacchaeus in response to Christ's love (241–286).

Son of God, Physician, Shepherd, Nurse, Hope of the wicked, Lord of the world: Jacob invokes all these titles of our Lord in his description of this pivotal moment in the *mimro* of what occurred in Zacchaeus's house. Though reproached by the crowds, Christ pursues iniquity there in order to forgive it and by repentance bring the iniquitous to righteousness. Zacchaeus's conversion was remarkable (287–330), and now the wedding feast, the banquet prophesied, occurs. The conversion of Zacchaeus offers to humanity once again to partake of the feast interrupted in Eden by the sin of Adam. And all whom Zacchaeus had plundered now benefit from his transformation at the feast. Beholding the Son, "in one hour" he restores all that he had stolen. Christ yoked (*kadneh*) him as an apostle and without delay he gave up one half of his goods to those in need, most likely those whom he had already exploited (331–366).

The outcry over the conversion of Zacchaeus was greater than at the resurrection of Lazarus. To this Jacob comments that conversion from perdition (*'abdânâ*) is a greater sign (*âtâ*) than resurrection from corruption (*sri*). Then he reiterates the significance of the feast. It was not sufficient for Zacchaeus and Christ to have met along the way. Only when He went into his house and ate bread was true repentance achieved. The banquet, wedding feast and anticipation of Christ's redemptive meal with his disciples, had achieved its purpose. It brought life and salvation to a son of Abraham, by means of His love—a new deed along Christ's way (*ûrḥâ*) (367–400).

THE MANUSCRIPT TRADITION

For his edition Bedjan employed London Br.Mus.Add.17159 and Vatican Syr.117 (12/13th century). Other manuscripts listed by Vööbus' <u>Überlieferung</u> II which contain the *mimro* are: Mardin Ortho.130, 133,135; Diyarbakir Mar Ja'qob 1/3; Paris Syr.117,196; Damascus Patr. 12/13, 12/14, 12/15.

SUMMARY

I. The Path of Christ's Mercy to heal the World (1–32).
II. The Power of Repentance Reflected in Zacchaeus as in a Mirror (33–72).
III. The Light of Grace Dawns in Zacchaeus' Soul (73–126).
IV. Zacchaeus Climbs up to gaze and the sight of the Lord fashions him anew (127–166).
V. The gaze of Zacchaeus at Christ is transfigured by Christ's love (167–202).
VI. Christ the Husbandman, by His teaching redeems the world (203–240).
VII. Zacchaeus as a First Fruit among Sinners (241–286).
VIII. The Lord of the world reclines in the house of Zacchaeus (287–330).

IX. At the great banquet, yoked by Christ, Zacchaeus begins to lavish his wealth upon the needy (331–366).
X. A soul restored from wickedness is a greater sign than a body's resurrection from destruction (367–400).

Text and Translation

THE PATH OF CHRIST'S MERCY
TO HEAL THE WORLD

1   For the sake of wicked humanity our Lord undertook His path[1] in the world,
indeed, to gather those who had wandered from His Father's house.

He directed His way to sinners so as to bring them back,   Ps 25:8, 51:3, 1 Tim 1:15

and He sought out the erring, that the lost might again be found.   Lk 15:2

5   In His zeal He left the found and sought after the lost: Mt 15:24, Lk 15:4, 19:10

He forsook the perfect and kept company with the repentant.

He was kissed by a harlot and He accepted it.   Lk 7:38

People invited Him along with sinners, and He took delight in it.

He was called a companion of tax-collectors and harlots;   Mt 11:19, Lk 5:29-31, 7:34, 15:31

---

[1] Path (*ûrḥâ*): Christ's way (*ûrḥâ*) is the will of the Father and he goes accordingly to perfect his work in order to accomplish his way, see Kollamparampil, *Salvation*, 261–63; 265–75. Soteriology thus becomes more important than Christology in defining Jacob's theology according to Rilliet, "La métaphore," p. 38. The term *ûrḥâ* is found throughout Jacob's *Letters*. It occurs in the *Acts of the Apostles* with a different emphasis. See also the *Odes of Solomon*: 7:2, 11:3, 17:9, 22:11, 24:13, 38:7, 39:7,13; 42:2.

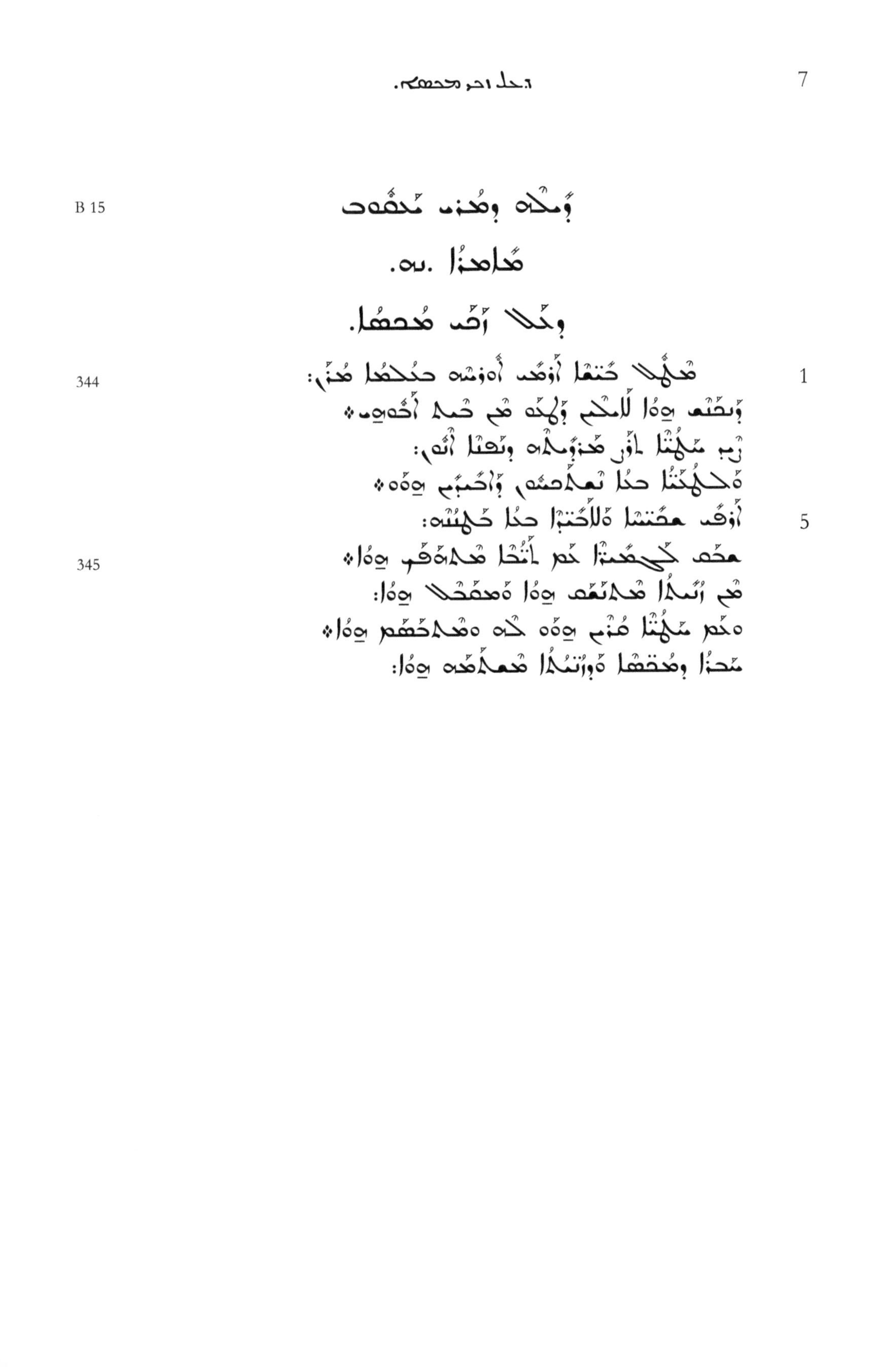

10	He carried bandages and showed love to none save the broken.	Lk 10:34
	The good Physician[2] did not come down to care for the healthy,	Cf. Mt 9:11, Mk 2:17, Lk 5.31
	since only the sickly were in need of His succour.	
	The one who is not dead has no need of resurrection,	
	and superfluous is forgiveness to one who has not sinned.	
15	He who is broken asks that a bandage be applied to him,	
	and one who is stricken calls a physician for healing.	
	The medicine for ulcerous wounds is applicable only to ulcerous wounds;	
	a prescription for disease is sought for by none save the diseased.	
	Only the broken of heart have need of encouragement,	Ps 34:18, 51:17, 147:3, Is 61:1
20	and likewise, only for the grieved in spirit is consolation necessary.	
	The one who has ulcers requires medicines,[3]	
	and with healing, he will have relief for his running sores.	
	The one who owes much loves Him to whom he is in debt,	Lk 7:41-3

---

[2] God as Physician (*âsyâ*) is found in the OT, Ex 15:26. In the N.T., Shemunkasho has noted seventy references to Jesus as the one who heals. And in Ephrem he shows the uses of the term *âsyâ* for Jesus: the heavenly Physician, the wise Physician, the great Physician, the good Physician, the pure Physician. See A. Shemunkasho, *Healing*, 119–40. See also Bou Mansour, *Jacques*, II, 114–25.

[3] Medicines (*sammâne*): a physician uses the medicines to reveal and to heal physical and spiritual wounds. Another meaning of the plural form is *pigments* which portray the image of the kingdom in the soul at Baptism. This contrasts with the corrupted image of Adam (*Hymns on Virginity* 7.5), an image in need of healing using medicines. See Shemunkasho, *Healing*, 140–47. This link between pigments and medicines indicates the richness in meaning of iconic imagery in Ephrem and in Jacob. See note 26.

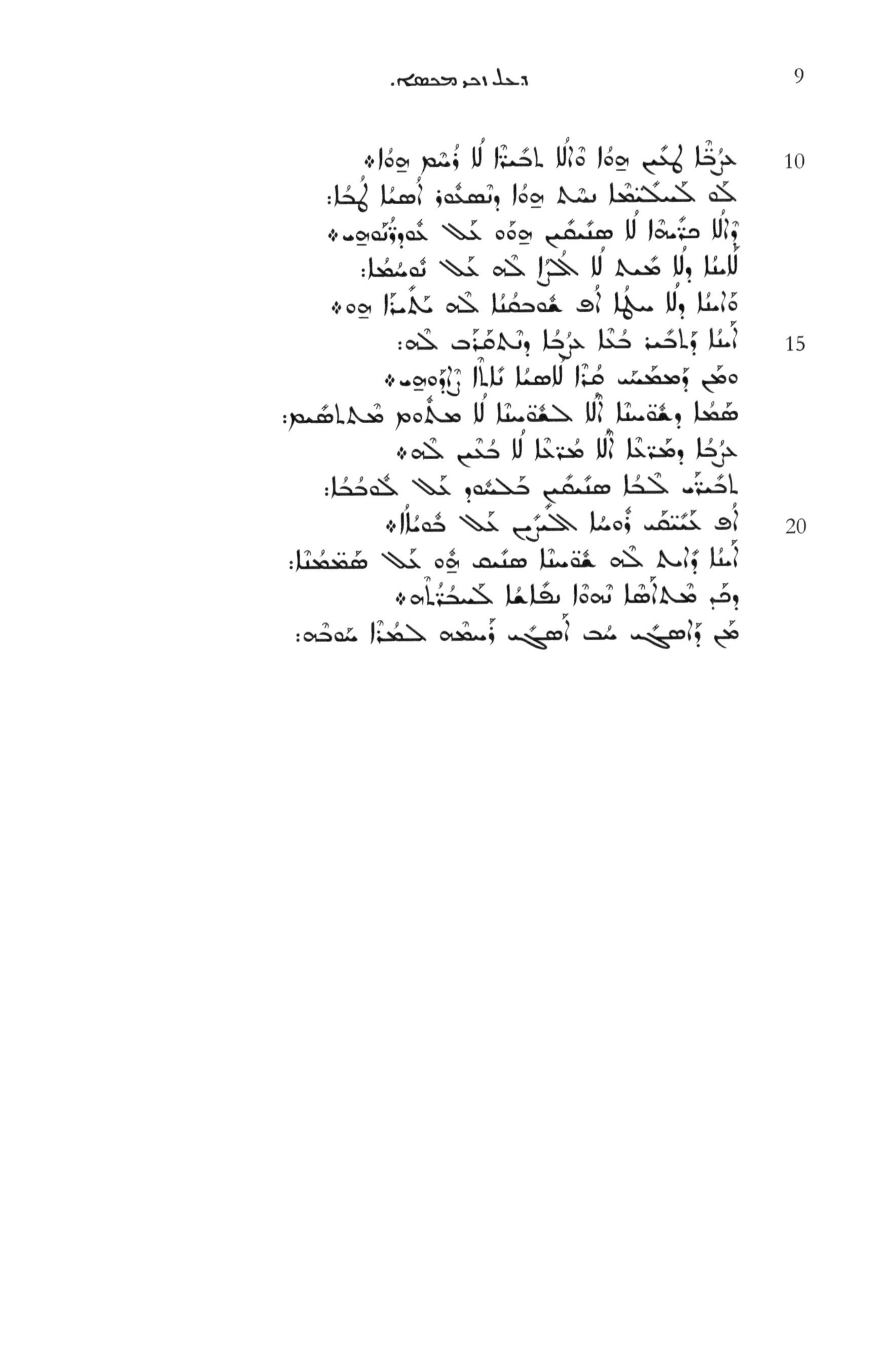

because his soul hangs upon forgiveness, of which he has great need.

25 The medicine of mercy will usefully be applied
only to the one whose soul has been stricken with iniquity and who suffers from the wound.

The one whom sin has bitten and who laments prudently
feels the need for the Doctor[4] who will devise a remedy.

The one whose members have been pierced by the arrow of wickedness
30 seeks for mercy that would extract the arrow-head of his passion.

The one upon whom sin has fallen like a lioness,
seeks for divine compassion which would rescue him from destruction.

POWER OF REPENTANCE REFLECTED IN ZACCHAEUS AS IN A MIRROR

Rightly, then, did our Saviour come to sinners
to care for them as a physician cares for the wounded.
35 In Zacchaeus the tax-collector, He made a market-place for repentance,[5]

---

[4] Doctor (*'âṣobâ*) sometimes used to refer to Christ the Physician, see Bou Mansour, *Éphrem*, 259–71.

[5] Repentance (*tyâbûtâ*): see Aphrahat, *Dem.* XV; Ephrem's homily "On Admonition and Repentance." Jacob has two homilies on repentance: Bedjan I, Hom. 28 and Hom.29. References to repentance are found throughout the O.T.: both of ceasing to do evil and of doing good. The rabbis have much to say about repentance. In the Talmud it is one of the seven things created before the world was created (Pes. 54a); it reaches up to the Throne of Glory (Yoma 86a); it prolongs life and brings on the Redemption (Yoma 86b). And in Midrash: an opening of repentance no bigger than the eye of a needle will yield a gate through which wagons and carriages can pass (Song Rabbah 5:2 no. 2). Neusner traces the development of a shift in thinking from propositional to symbolic discourse during the 5th and 6th cent., in the Babylonian Talmud and in midrashic literature, especially *Song of Songs Rabbah*. A comparison of Ephrem/Jacob and the rabbis on repentance might yield further insights. See Neusner, *Symbol and Theology*.

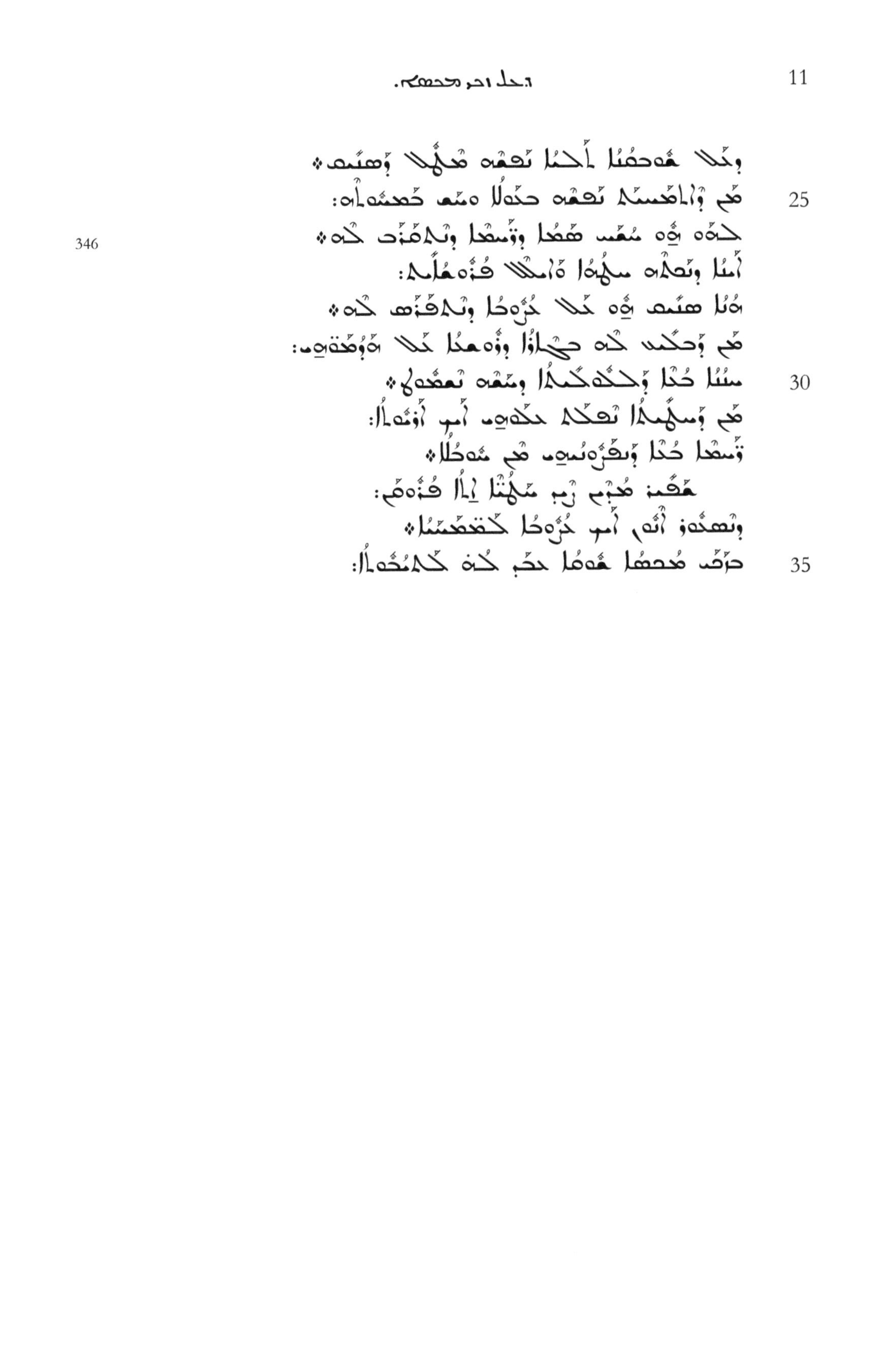

so that every man might come and trade therein without hindrance.

By that plunderer He gave encouragement to iniquitous ones,
that if they should repent, they would not be punished by justice.

He placed him as a mirror[6] before the eyes of others, that they study him
40 and learn that if they convert, their faults will be forgiven.

Who will despair of himself when he gazes at Zacchaeus,
the comrade of tax-collectors who became a comrade to the apostles?[7]

Who will think his faults unforgivable
when he sees the extortioner joined with the disciples?

45 Who will not run to take refuge in repentance,
wherein lies power that makes even hawks into doves?

Who will not follow this good Shepherd,[8]
who traps wolves so as to make them sheep in His flock?

Who so hates his own life as to flee from
50 this Physician whose power triumphs over all wounds?

---

[6] Mirror (*maḥzitâ*). Here Zacchaeus is offered as a mirror to bring about repentance. The mirror reflects divine reality, and the interior eye illumined by faith is able to see God's action in it. In his *Letters*, Jacob says that the way of life of the saints is a mirror, see Olinder p. 297. Mirror imagery occurs already in the Odes of Solomon and in the Acts of Thomas but the term is most frequent in Ephrem for whom *maḥzitâ* may be found throughout Scripture and Nature. Bou Mansour considers it to be one of the key terms in Ephrem's symbolic theology together with *râzâ*, *dmûtâ*, *ṣalmâ*, *peletâ*, and *nišâ*. See Bou Mansour, *Éphrem*, 23–71. Ephrem's most extended use of mirror imagery is in his "Letter to Publius." For an overview of *maḥzitâ*, see S.P. Brock, "The Imagery of the Spiritual Mirror in Syriac Literature," *JCSSS* 5(2005) 3–17.

[7] Lit. "to apostleship".

[8] Shepherd (*râ'yâ*): see R. Murray, *Symbols*, 187–191, including uses of the term as applied to Apostles and bishops.

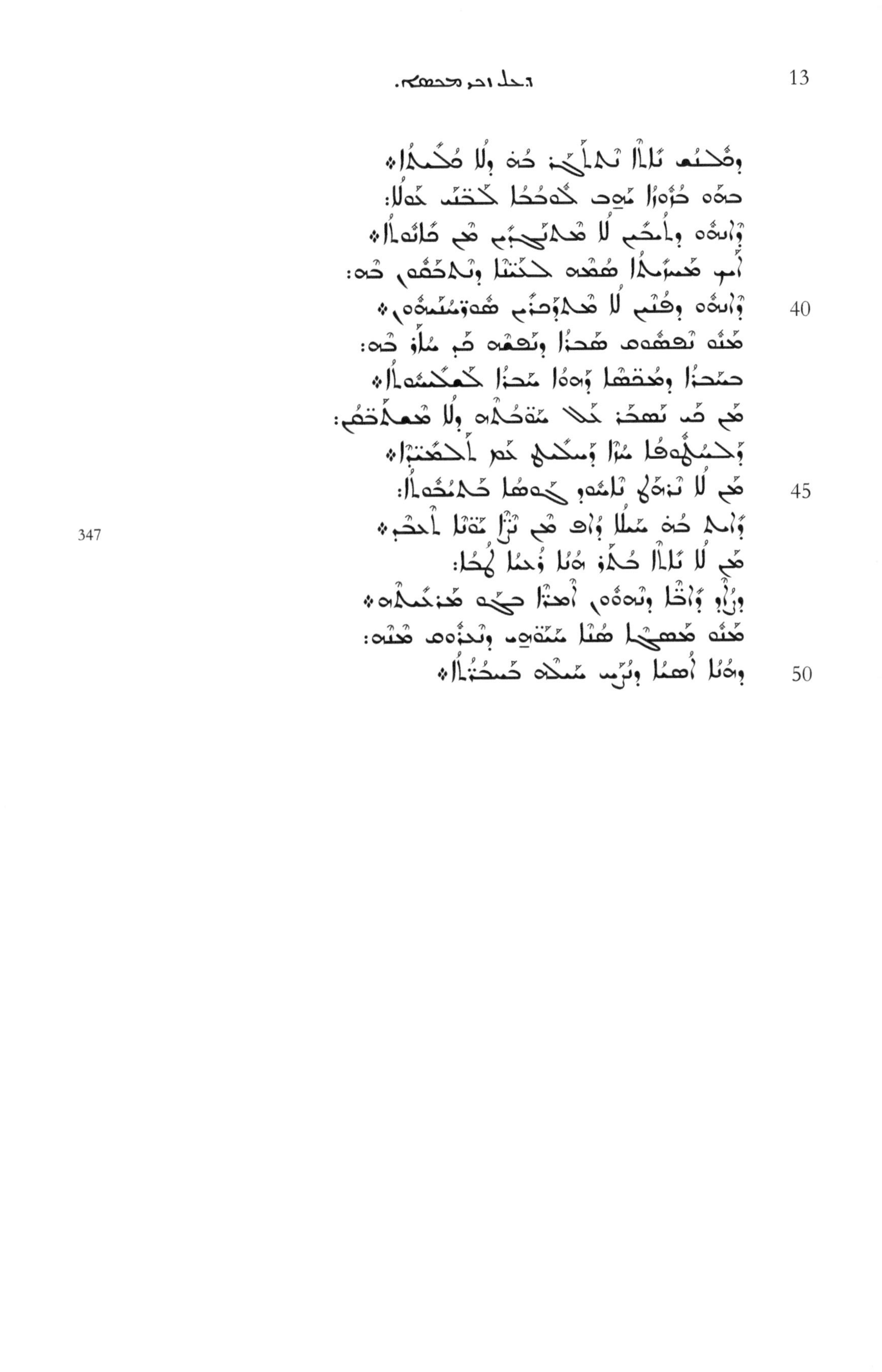

He mingled the tax-collector with the disciples as a device,
setting bait for all extortioners, that they might imitate him.
Who would not marvel at what the Son of God caught—
the greedy tax-collector, who was to become an apostle to the repentant?

55 This one, whose rapacious house was filled with groaning,[9]
who repeatedly amassed the spoil of others' possessions;
this one, who snatched from merchants whatsoever he could,
and who knew not how to live without rapacity;
this one sinned without shame all the days of his life,
60 being supported by the law and governmental authority.
While sinning he was confident and, exercising authority,
he wrought iniquity, and doing so was unabashed.
His sin was evident, yet left unprosecuted by the judges;
his wickedness was known, and they did not restrain him because it was his work.
65 The work of the tax-collector and the harlot is manifest wickedness;
he does not hide under an outward show to prevent exposure;
he forcefully seizes without shame as others look on;
he freely plunders without blushing as they behold him.
This is sin which defies both shame and law,
70 and is unconcealed from onlookers when it is perpetrated.

---

[9] I.e. the groaning of the persons he unjustly treated.

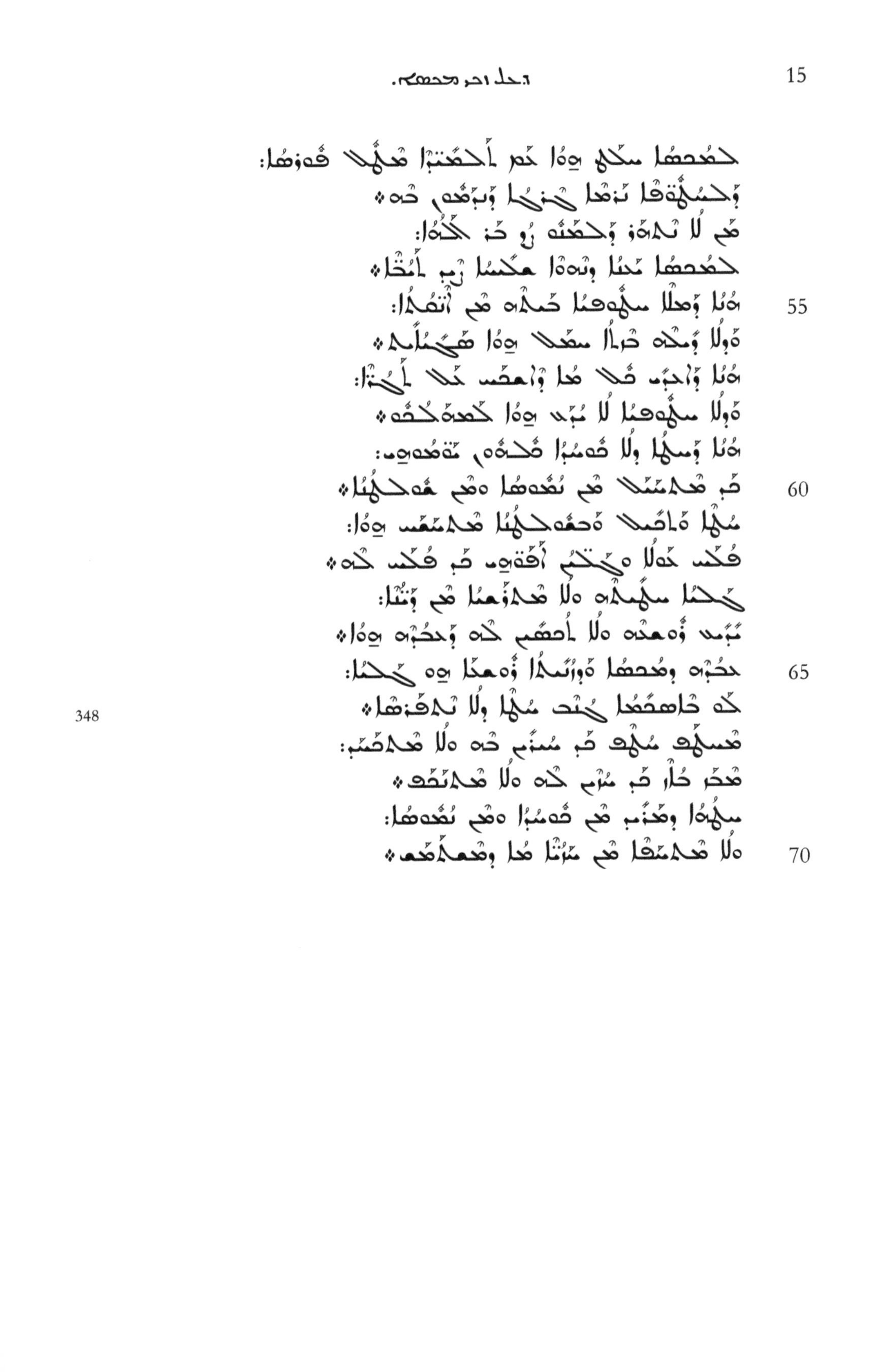

The iniquity of the tax-collector is loudly proclaimed before whoever encounters him,
it is robbery daily re-enacted in all its forms.

THE LIGHT OF GRACE DAWNS IN ZACCHAEUS' SOUL

Zacchaeus the tax-collector heard that Jesus was passing through the land of Judea,
and with love he wisely went out after Him to see Him.

75 He was ill with iniquity, and he heard news that the Physician was coming;
carrying his sickness, he went forth to see Him, that by chance He might heal him.

Having in his soul a great consuming wound,
he hastened to go to the medicinal Herb of Life,[10] our very Lord.

Avarice beheld the Just One and shut its mouth;
80 with wholesome thoughts it stood up to scrutinize Him.

The plunderer heard that, behold, the upright Judge was passing by,
and he left off the habitual practices in which he was engaged.

From grace, light dawned in Zacchaeus' soul,
and he recognized that in the Son, who forgives debts, he might take refuge.

85 He entered into repentance as into a walled city
to seek shelter from a robber's marauding power.

The lost sheep heard tidings of the Shepherd who had come,
and he ran after Him to include himself into His flock.

He saw the crowds which closely surrounded Him,

---

[10] Medicinal Herb of Life (*'eqârâ d-ḥaye*): Christ is both Physician and Medicinal Herb for the wounds of humanity. See Kollamparampil, *Salvation*, 339–40.

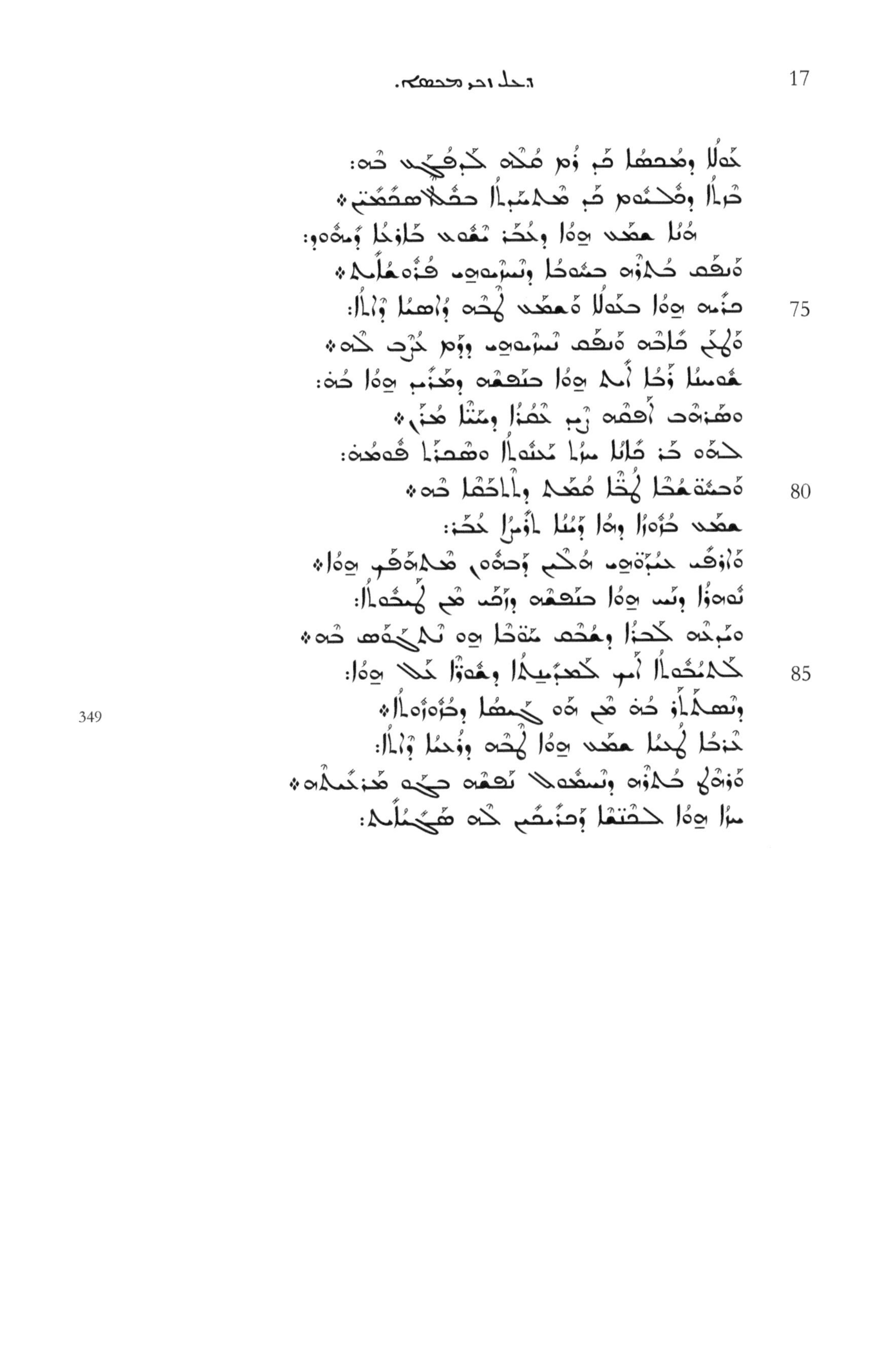

90 and the ranks of people which surged on forcefully ahead of Him.

He strained to see the Son, but the multitudes
which pressed forward from all sides to keep near Him, did not allow him.

He was little of stature, the people thronged together, and what should he do?

His pain was intense, but the Physician was concealed from his sight.

95 He was afflicted by sins and longed to see Him who came to care for the suffering;
*********************************** [11]

The little man was hemmed in by the great concourse
and did not manage to see the Son whom he loved.

Though Zacchaeus was small in his appearance,
100 not so small was his love, which surpassed even the world in breadth and width.

Though his stature was smaller than those surrounding him,
his mind transcended even the clouds, because he loved.

If you look with discernment at this man,
you will perceive him to be one of the mighty and renowned by reason of his lofty intellect.

105 A great soul in a little body was to be seen,
one whose measure transcended created things and their formations.[12]

His limbs were small, but his thoughts were far-reaching;
his appearance was little, but in searching he was greater than many.

---

[11] The second verse of the couplet seems to be missing.
[12] Formations (*tûqânayhen*).

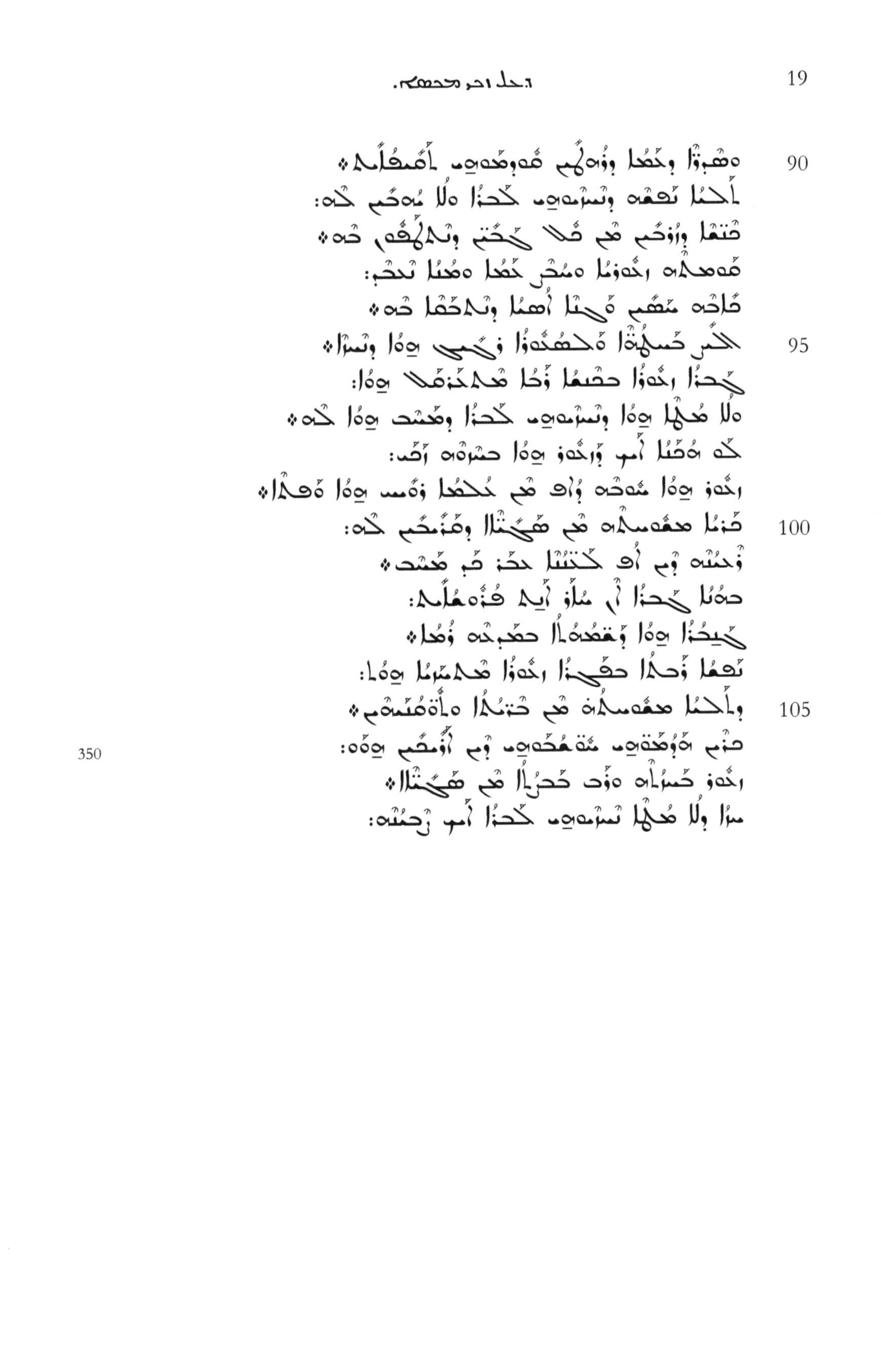

He perceived that he would not succeed in seeing the
    Son as he wished,
110   and so the wise one ran to a fig tree[13] to find a means.

Immediately Zacchaeus said the following to the fig
    tree:

"Make a way[14] for me, as you have been accustomed
    to do from the beginning of time!

You clothed Adam when he was stripped: Gen.3:7
now provide for my need, that I may see the Son.

115   Allow me to scale your height that, standing in your
    boughs,
I may catch sight of the Lord of Eden who has come
    to visit us.

Make a place[15] for me in your lofty crest where I may
    stand and see
Him who, with His Father, caused all trees to sprout.

Briefly bear me up while I gaze upon and scrutinize
120   the Fruit of Life[16] which was sent to us from on high.

My stature is small, and if I stand not upon your
    height,
I shall not catch sight of thy Lord amid the crowds.

I have no height, and you have no fruit, since you are
    barren:
be height for me, and I shall be your fruit.

---

[13] Fig tree (*têtâ*): Jesus had dried up the fig tree (Mt. 21:19) since he had come to heal Adam, and its leaves (Gen. 3:7) were no longer needed as He was bringing a robe of glory to clothe him. From this very tree renewed by Christ's suffering, Jacob sees Zacchaeus as a first fruit. See Jacob's *mimro* "On the Fig Tree which Our Lord Cursed," Bedjan IV, 724–39. See Ephrem, CD XVI.1–10 and his *Paradise Hymns*: II.7, III.13, VII.6, XI.8, XII.10.13.14. See also note 31.

[14] Way (*pursâ*).

[15] Place (*atrâ*): perhaps an intentional use of the Syriac term here. In his commentary to the "Homily on Zacchaeus" by Cyrillona, Vona sees the tree in Lk. 19 to be the Tree of Life in Paradise and he includes a reference to the Cross which would make of it a place (*atrâ*) of God's presence. On *atrâ* in Jacob, see note 36.

[16] Fruit of Life (*pirâ d-ḥaye*): "All the negative results of the fall are seen as blotted out by Christ who is depicted by symbolic titles such as the Fruit of Life." See Kollamparampil, *Salvation*, 115–16.

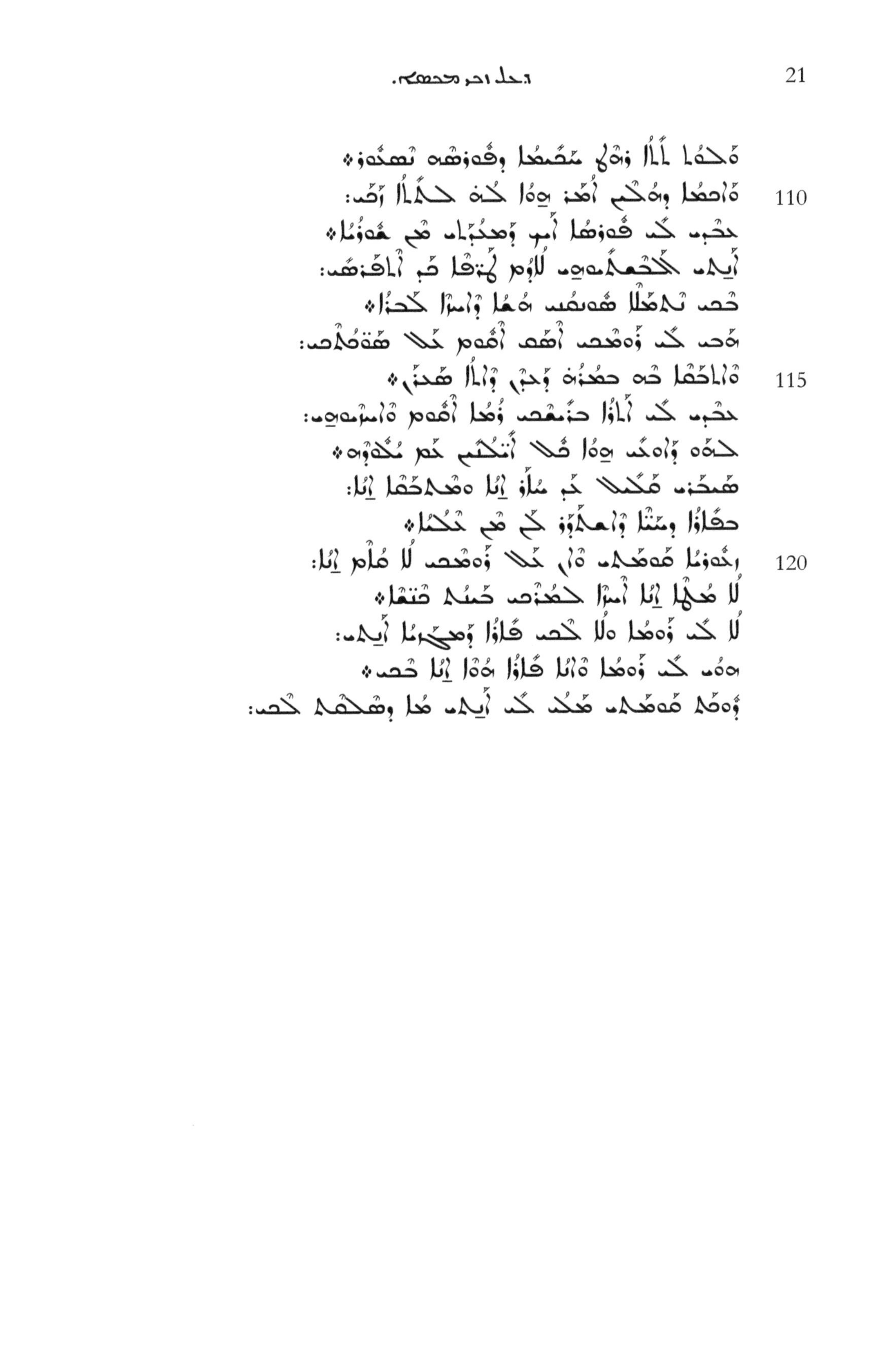

125   Fill up the deficiency of my stature when I climb upon you,
and I shall fill up for you the place of fruit."

Zacchaeus Climbs Up to Gaze and the Sight of the Lord Fashions Him Anew

Then the wise one climbed up and stood in the fig tree,
and see, he beheld our Lord who was coming, surrounded by the multitudes.

His short stature did not suffice his faith,
130   and so he added a borrowed height to himself so as to see the Son.

Love seized him, and he climbed up and stood in the tree,
that his vision might take its fill of the Son of God.

He perceived that he was lowly and would not be able to see the Son,
so he snatched a height not his own, on which he stood and saw Him.

135   His faith made for him a new stature
which, for a moment, was taller than the entire throng.

The lowly one climbed up and stood high in the tree
to view how much the Lofty One had descended unto lowliness.

He raised himself up to see Him who had descended;
140   he scaled the height to gaze upon Him who had come down to the depths.

The chief tax-collector looked upon our Lord and became righteous;
he saw Him from afar and loved Him as though from near at hand.

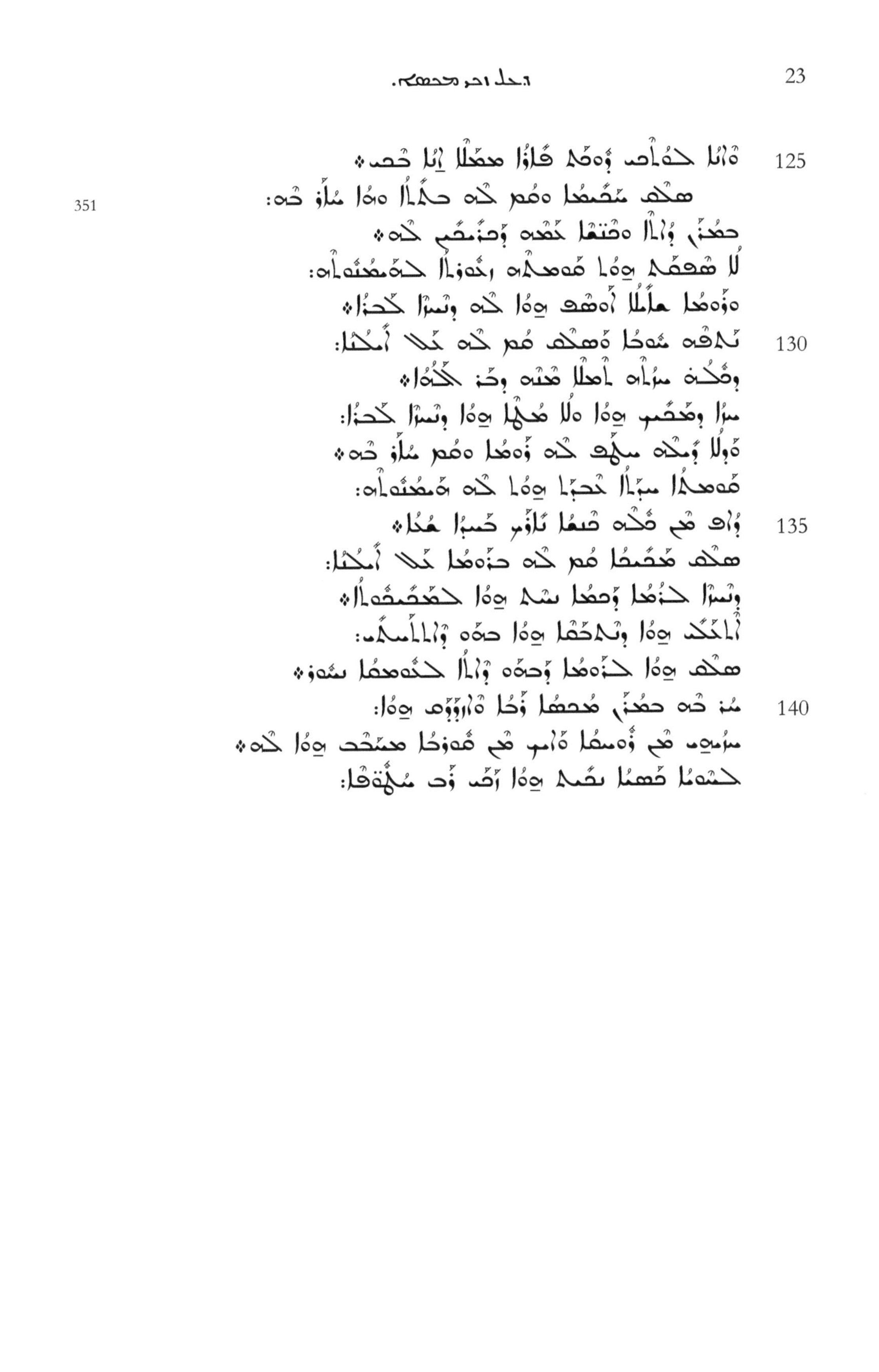

	Zacchaeus, the chief of the extortioners, had been bitten by a hidden serpent:	Num 21:6
	he gazed upon the Son, and its venom vanished from his members.[17]	Cf. Num 21:9
145	The viper's bite pained him when he perceived it, and he ran to look upon Him by whose type[18] the Hebrews were restored to life.	Num 21:9, Cf. Jn 3:14, 8:28, 12:32
	Our Lord stood in place of that bronze serpent for the chief tax-collector whom iniquity had bitten like a basilisk.	
150	Sin, like venom, was spread throughout his soul, but when he gazed upon the Son, it vanished from him and he became righteous.	Num 21:4-9
	The sight of our Lord fashioned[19] the tax-collector anew, for as soon as he looked upon Him, he was changed from his evil ways.	
	He merely gazed at Him, and he found all righteousness,	
155	for love produces action wherever it wishes to gaze.[20]	

---

[17] Zacchaeus inherited the venom from the serpent's having bitten Adam. It was Jesus' suffering which healed Adam's wound. And as Zacchaeus looked on Jesus he was healed, a healing prefigured by the presence of the bronze serpent in the desert. See Jacob's *mimro* "The Bronze Serpent" (Hom. 4, Bedjan I 47–67). Theodore of Mopsuestia in his "Preface to the Commentary on Jonah" speaks about the bronze serpent and its typological aspects. See also Narsai's "Memra on the Brazen Serpent." See J. Frishman, "Type and Reality."

[18] Type (*râzeh*), see Bou Mansour, *Éphrem*, 26–35.

[19] Zacchaeus looks on Jesus and is healed of his sinfulness, Christ created him anew. On healing as a second creation in Ephrem see Shemunkasho, *Healing*, 411–13.

[20] Love (*ḥûbâ*) occurs frequently in this homily, mostly from 154 to 180. Love and desire characterize how Jacob sees human understanding of God's providence. Zacchaeus knows because he loves not because he inquires or searches out. Whereas for Ephrem the key is faith, for Jacob it seems to be love. See Bou Mansour, *Jacques*, II, 411–24. See also S.P. Brock, "Dieu Amour." And on love as a key to the understanding of Scripture see Jacob's *mimro* "On the Veil of Moses" (Bed. vol. 3, Hom. 79, 283–305), lines 19–20.

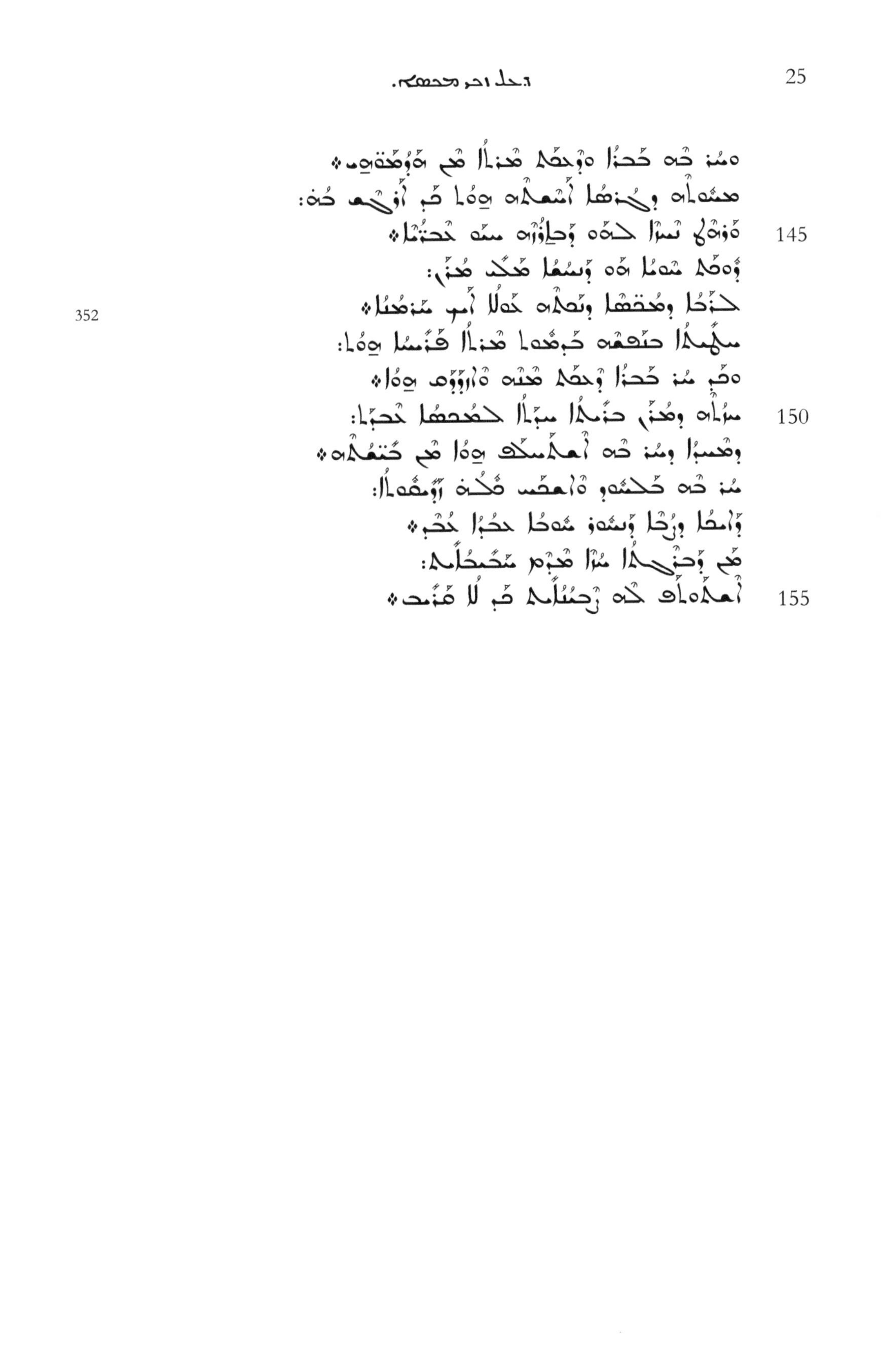

The one who with desire looks on something lovingly
voluntarily communes with it, though he be far off.

The impulses of desire bring about a work[21] after the manner of God
which causes either edification or destruction to him who possesses it.[22]

And evil desire produces iniquity even by its gaze,
160 whereas a desire of truth is entirely involved with God.

From the tree Zacchaeus saw God with desire,
and the fervour of his love joined him to Him in communion.

If one's soul desires to view something closely,
that thing is near at hand because of his love, however distant it may be.

165 There is no distance which can prevent desire from intermingling,[23]
for to the degree that it gazes, it is wholly joined with that which it beholds.

THE GAZE OF ZACCHAEUS AT CHRIST IS TRANSFORMED BY CHRIST'S LOVE

Zacchaeus stood further away than the entire throng,
but because he gazed at Christ with desire, he was joined to Him.

The fire of love burned hotly within him,
170 and as he looked upon the Son, with desire he received Him into his thoughts.

If love had not performed its work there,
who would have been further from our Saviour than Zacchaeus?

---

[21] Work (*britâ*).
[22] I.e. the desire or the work
[23] Intermingling (*ḥûltânâ*) and joined (*ḥlîtâ*): words of mingling in Jacob reflect the Incarnation. Along His way (*ûrḥâ*) He mingles with creation. See Kollamparampil, *Salvation* 199–200. For metaphors of mingling and mixing in early Syriac literature, see Stewart, '*Working the Earth of the Heart*,' 188–203.

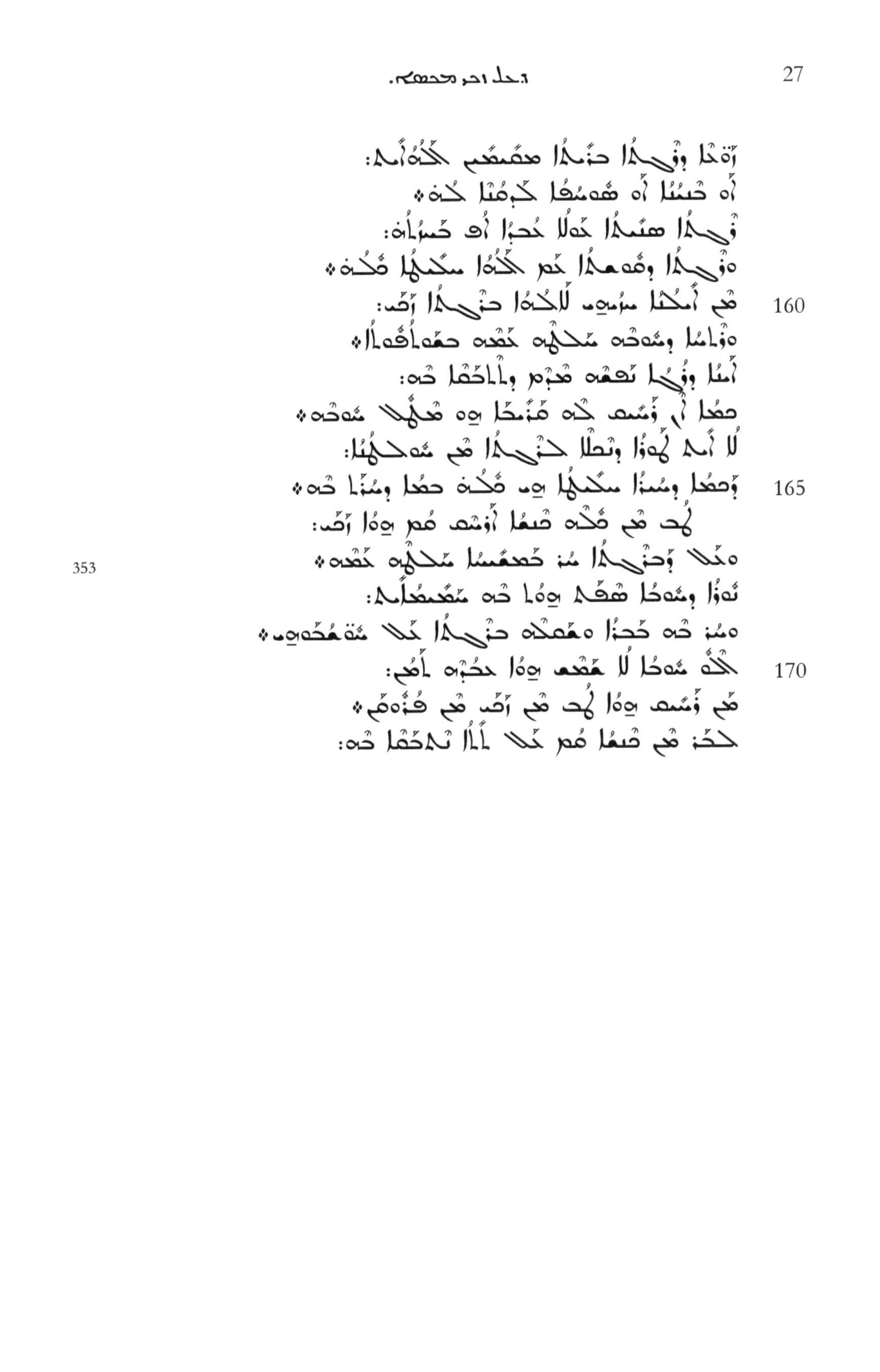

> Outside the crowd he stood in the fig tree to look upon Him,
> but his love brought him nearer than all who were assembled there.

175 He gazed while loving, he beheld the Son while yearning,
> and who was there that was so close to Him as he?

> As his thirsty gaze knelt down toward our Saviour,
> drinking from Him as from a wellspring full of life;

> and as he snatched the Son from amid the throng with his eyes,

180 that he alone might take delight in Him, that Sweet Fruit;[24]

> and as he rejoiced to have found a place according to his wish,
> high enough that from it he might see Him whom he loved:

> then our Lord looked up into the tree as He was passing
> and saw Zacchaeus standing in its boughs.

185 He looked upon him with love and began to say to him:
> "Come, Zacchaeus, I see you as you see Me.

> Come, tax-collector, and be an apostle to the repentant,
> and teach them that I possess mercy along with forgiveness.

> Come, O sinner, go out together with My disciples and proclaim Me,

190 for I receive whoever repents of his evil deeds.

---

[24] Sweet Fruit (*pirâ ḥalyâ*): for the Christological dimensions of *pirâ* see Bou Mansour, *Jacques*, II, 101–09. The relation of Fruit to the Tree or Root is examined by Ephrem in his *Hymns on Faith* 77. And Bou Mansour looks at the Trinitarian aspects of this imagery in his *Éphrem*, 187–93.

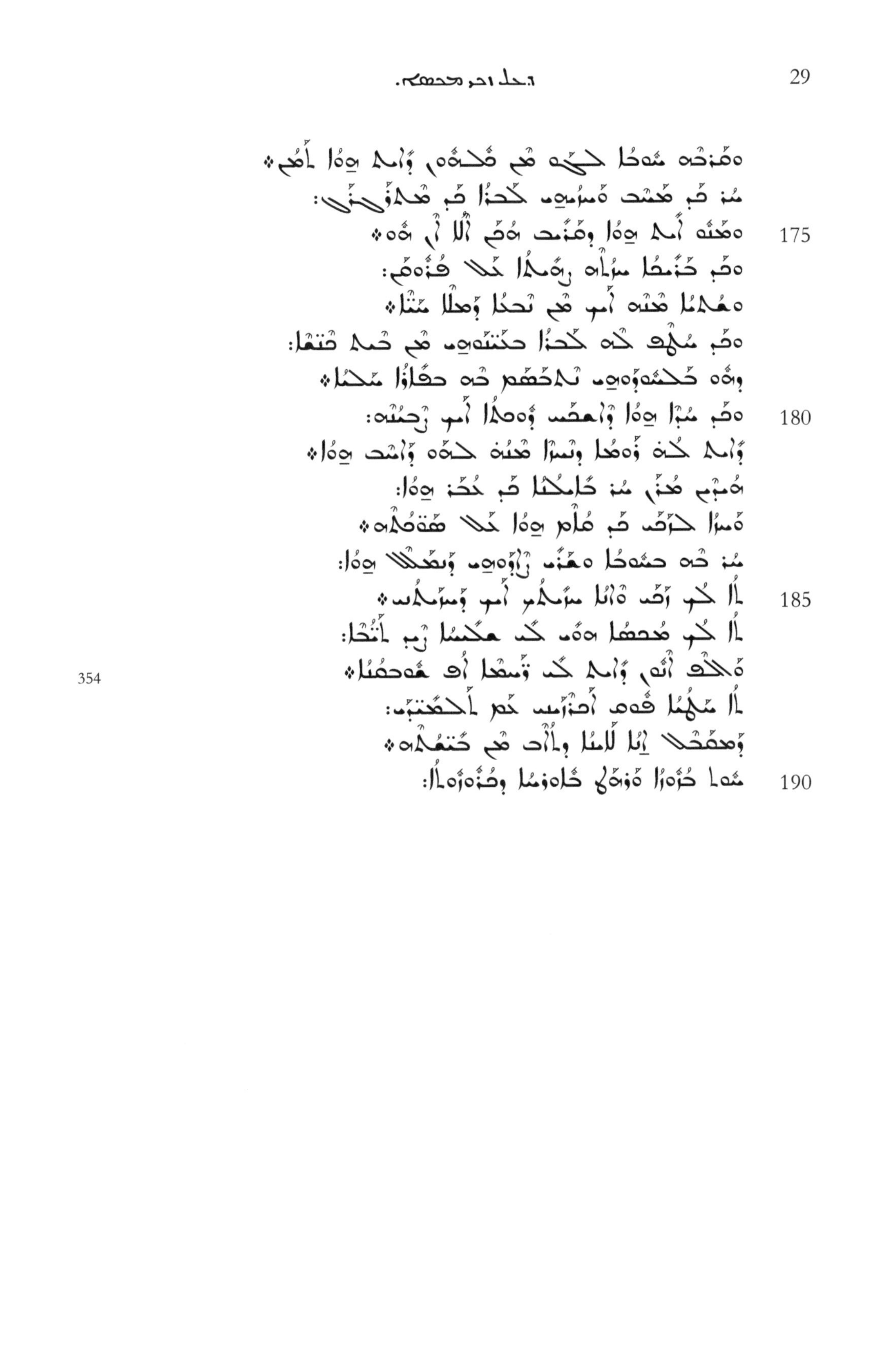

Come down, plunderer, and hasten on the path of preaching:
proclaim hope and life to the wicked with a resounding voice.

Come, I shall send you to the lawless to teach them
that I possess mercy and I receive the one who seeks Me.

195 Come, I shall portray in you a comely image[25] of repentance,
so that the whole world may admire and imitate you.[26]

Come, be among sinners an advocate of My compassion,
that I earnestly wish to forgive the debts of whomever seeks Me.

In you peoples, worlds, and regions will learn of Me,
200 that I am the Shepherd, and that I cherish the lost sheep. Lk 15:4-6, 24, 19:10, Jn 10:11

Come, descend, Zacchaeus: I must abide in your house today; Lk 19:5
come down, make ready for Me, that I may take pleasure at your repast."

Christ the Husbandman, by His Teaching Redeems the World

This was a guest who came of His own bidding,
and though He was not invited, He was ready for a supper.

---

[25] Portray (*eṣûr*): Ephrem's use of visual imagery to depict the economy of salvation is well documented in Sidney Griffith's "The Image of the Image Maker in the Poetry of St. Ephraem the Syrian." The verb *ṣûr* is found in Bou Mansour's study of Ephrem's use of symbols, another indication that iconic imagery may be very basic to Ephrem's way of theologizing, see Bou Masour, *Éphrem*, 44–52. For examples in Jacob see Konat's "A Metrical Homily of Jacob of Serugh." Here words like image, picture, depiction, color, carve, draw, imprint are found throughout. Kollamparampil comments on Jacob's iconic imagery, see *Salvation*, 391–93.

[26] Here Zacchaeus becomes an effective sign for all humanity much as did the Sinful Woman, see Johnson, "The Sinful Woman," 71, 81.

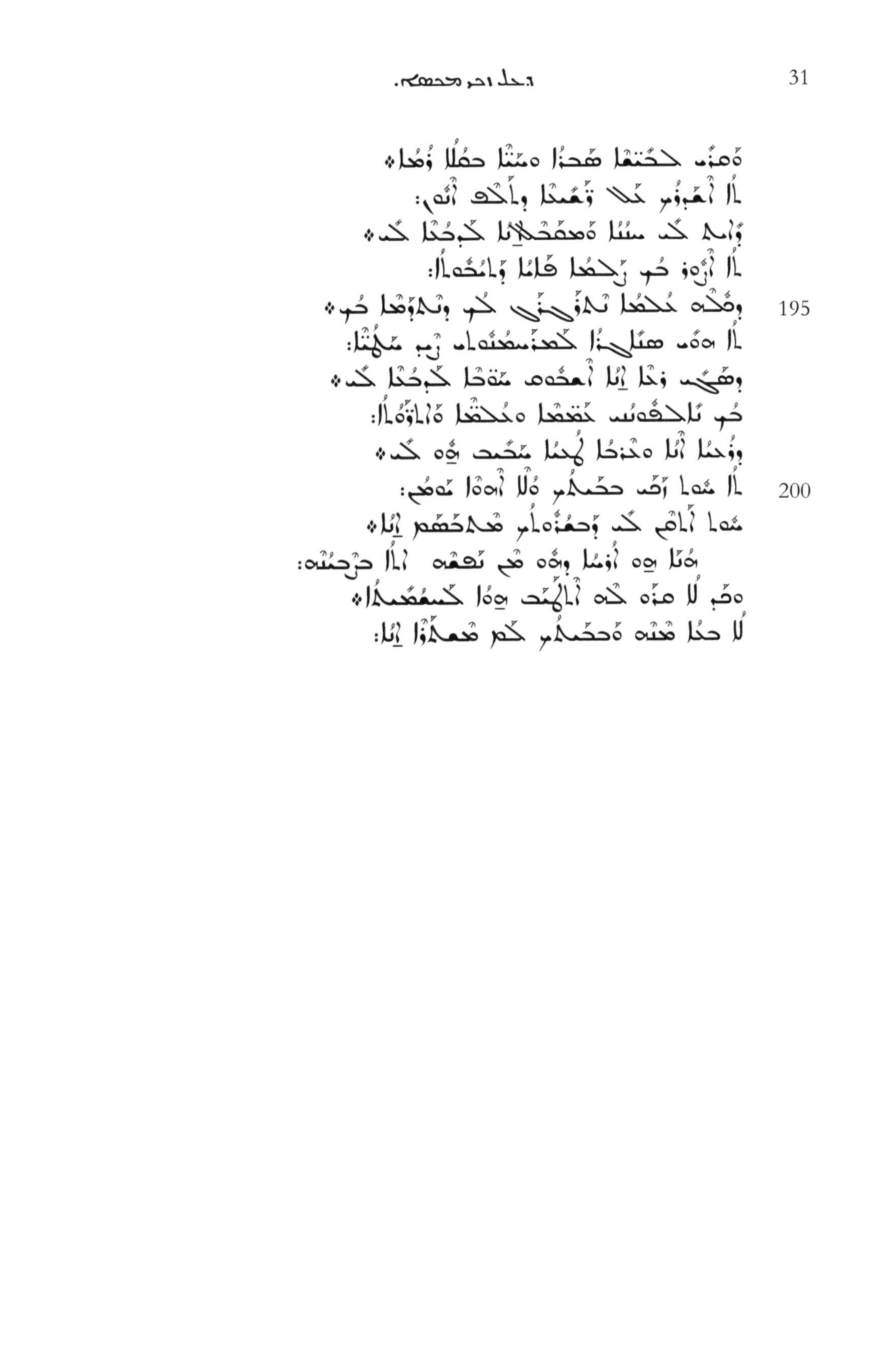

205	He did not ask Zacchaeus, but said, 'In your house I must lodge'²⁷:
	love gazed upon Him and exceedingly rejoiced to go with Him.
	O Husbandman,²⁸ who cultivated a field which was overgrown,
	labouring until even the weeds were turned into stalks of wheat!
	The irrigation of His teaching kept the wicked thorns low
210	until they produced sweet fruit throughout the world.
	From a harlot He received tears as a first fruit, *(Hos 9:10, Js 1:18, Rev 14:4)*
	and the chief tax-collector, who simply gazed at Him, He made an apostle.
	Even from stones He brought forth fruit by His crucifixion,²⁹ *(Mt 27:51-3, Lk 19:40)*
	and flinty rocks issued streams for Him when He required it of them. *(Ex 17:5ff, Deut 8:15, 1 Cor 10:4)*
215	In the wilderness He gave bread, in inhabited regions good wine, *(Ex 16:31, Deut 8:16, Jn 2:1-11)*
	to the hungry satiety, and to the suffering every kind of succour. *(Ex 3:7, Mt 15:32-7)*
	He passed not through a place without receiving tribute there, *(Mt 22:15-22)*
	and even the barren fig tree He required to give Him fruit.

---

²⁷ Lodge (*meštare*): for this and other images of dwelling and the indwelling of Christ as found in early Syriac literature derived from *šrâ*, see Stewart, '*Working the Earth of the Heart,*' 211–23.

²⁸ Husbandman ('*akârâ*): see Murray, *Symbols*, 195–99. Included are references to the *Odes of Solomon*, to Aphrahat and to Ephrem.

²⁹ The shaking of the earth and the splitting of the rocks in Mt. 27:51–53 are seen by Jacob, as well as by Ephrem and Narsai, as cosmic praise. See Jacob's Homily on the Sunday of the Hosannas 171–204 and his Prose Homily on the Sunday of the Hosannas 43–46 in Kollamparampil, *Select Festal Homilies*. Ephrem says that this cry of the stones was announced in Lk. 19:40. For textual references in Ephrem and in Narsai see Rilliet, "La Louange des Pierres et le Tonerre."

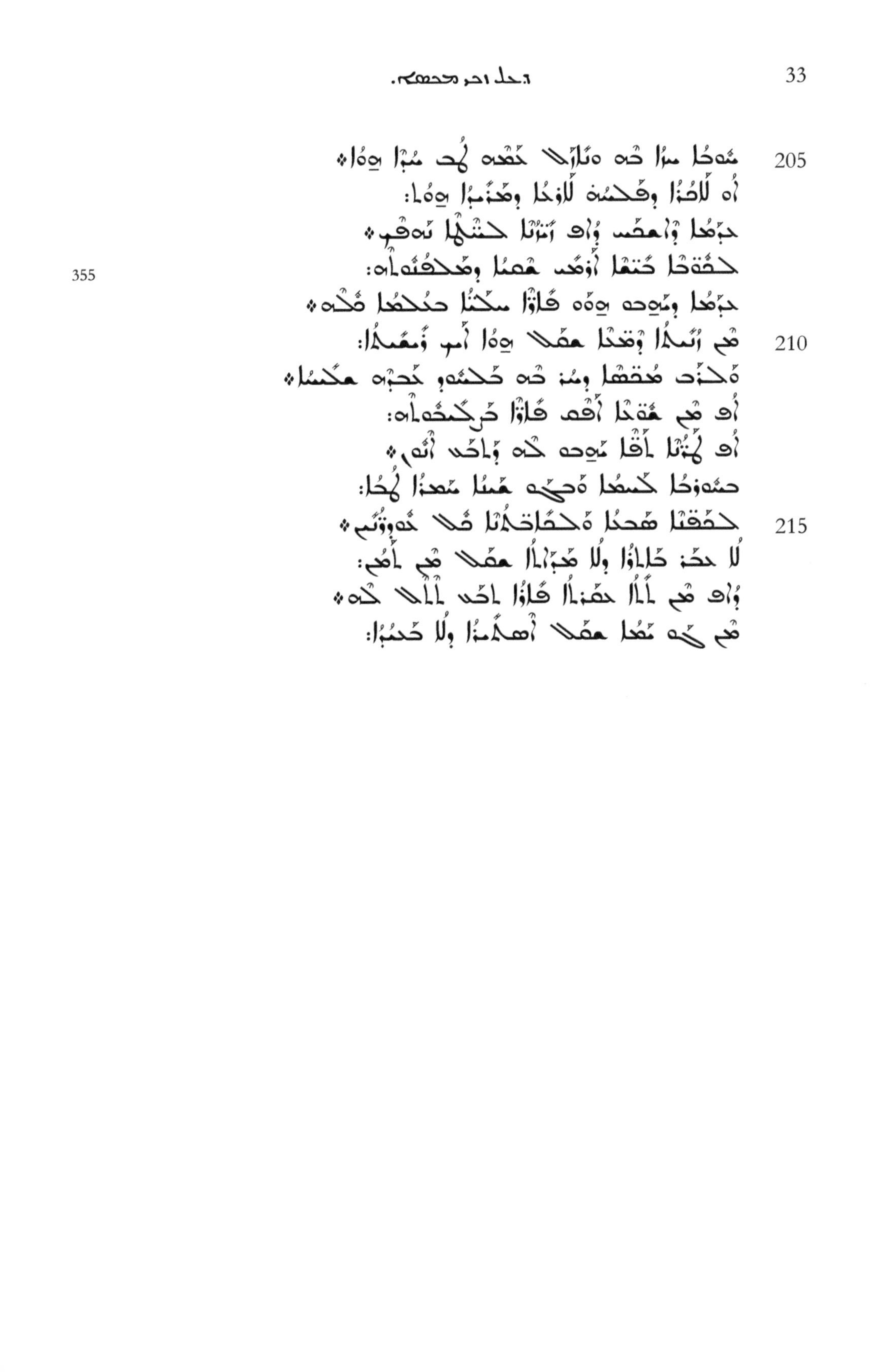

	From out of the sea He received a coin in an unusual manner,[30]	Mt 17:24-7
220	and from that unfruitful tree He received a sweet fruit.	
	Beloved was the fruit of the flavourless fig tree[31]	
	which Christ plucked from its branches as He passed.	
	He saw Zacchaeus in the tree like a ripe first fruit,	Hos 9:10, James 1:18, Rev 14:4
	and quickly plucked him so as to make use of his sweet savour.	
225	Not even in Eden did He once find a fruit like this one,	
	which He plucked from that fig tree as He passed through Jericho.	
	Zacchaeus was not like Adam, who fled among the trees	
	and took leaves from the fig tree, but nothing else.	
	Rather, he yearned to see the Son from the tree,	
230	and resembled not Adam, who endeavoured to hide himself from the Creator.	
	He was ripe with love and full of the savour of repentance,[32]	
	attaining even to the degree of being delightful to God.	
	From Jericho and from that unsavoury fig tree	
	Christ, by His skill, produced this fruit.	
235	The desolate city and the tree bereft of produce	

---

[30] See Ephrem CD XIV, 16–17, where all creation comes with first fruits as tribute.

[31] Throughout this *mimro* Jacob ignores an equivalent in Syriac, *têtâ pkihtâ*, insipid fig or sycamore. (The Greek text 19:4 uses sycamore, taking the word as a compound *sukos* fig + *moros* stupid). But here and in 233, he uses *pkihtâ* to describe its fruit. Elsewhere he uses only *têtâ* which has been translated as fig tree. See note 13.

[32] Savour of repentance (*ta'mâ d-tyâbûtâ*) for the impact of sensory experience in Christian life, not as a metaphor but as a way of knowing, see S. Harvey, "St. Ephrem on the Scent of Salvation"; see also her "Embodiment in Time and Eternity: a Syriac perspective."

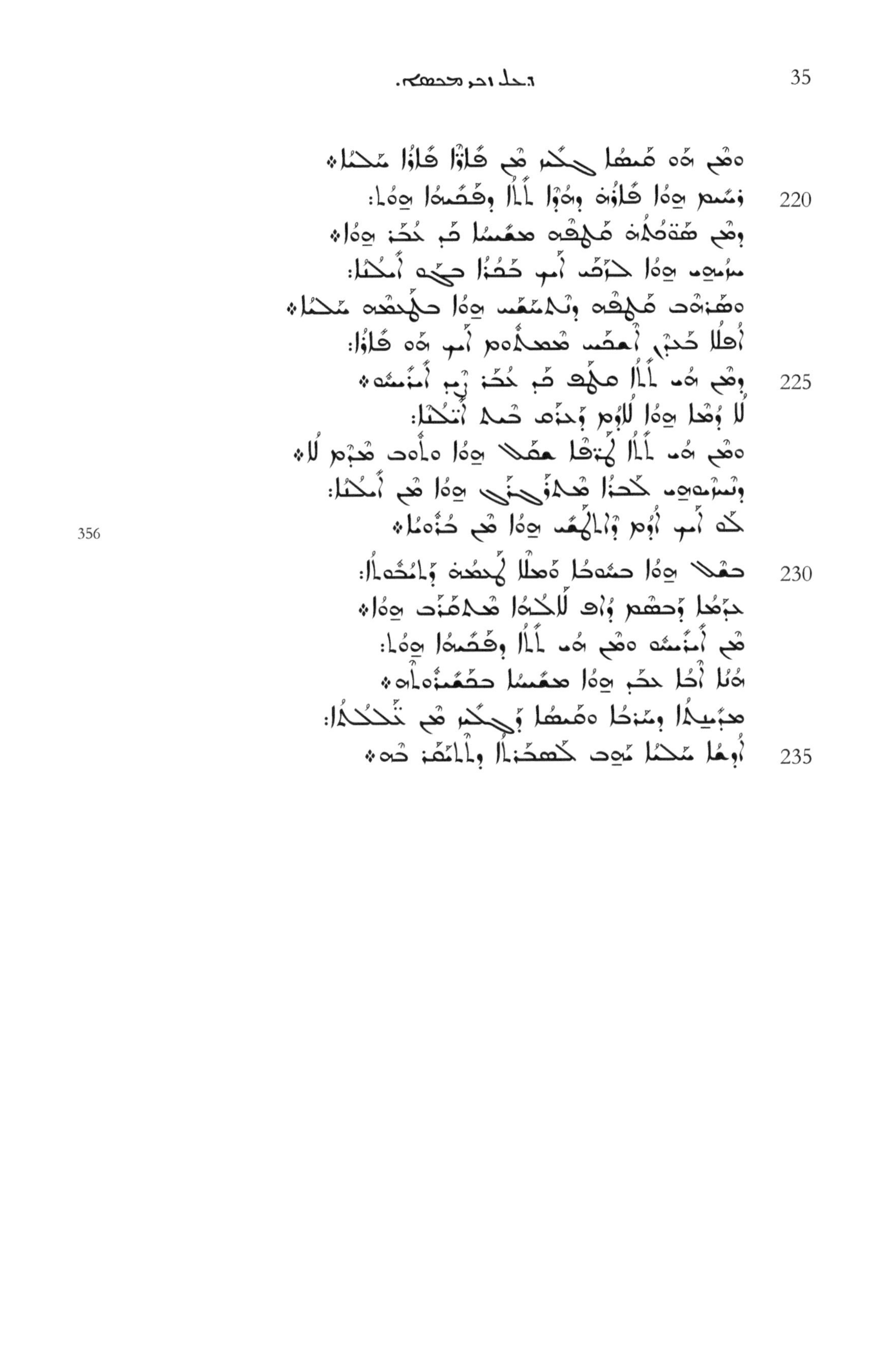

yielded a sweet crop for the Gospel whereby it would receive honour.

Great is the power of repentance when it shines forth: by its strength it can even rebuild the desolate.

In one which bore no crop at all, repentance produced fruit,

240 on a barren tree it suspended a cherished cluster in Jericho.

ZACCHAEUS AS A FIRST FRUIT AMONG SINNERS

The Son of God wrought new deeds on the path He journeyed,[33]

and by every means He trapped the world into repentance.

He took Zacchaeus as a first fruit from among sinners, — Hos 9:10, James 1:18, Rev 14:4

that he might become a pattern[34] for whomever should draw nigh to repentance.

245 "Come, descend, Zacchaeus", and he, the prudent one, hurried to climb down,

and, with a sincere heart, to receive the Lord of kings.

He was eager to bring into his house the great wealth he encountered,

for he did not suppose that he would ever find such a treasure.

The eye of the covetous tax-collector rested upon a Merchant,

250 and he led Him so as to bring Him to plunder from Him great riches.

He saw a load of mercies passing by there on the road,

and he desired to bring it in, that it might remain in his house.

A caravan came down bearing mercy from on high:

---

[33] path (*ûrḥâ*).
[34] pattern (*nîšâ*): see Bou Mansour, *Éphrem*, 57–61.

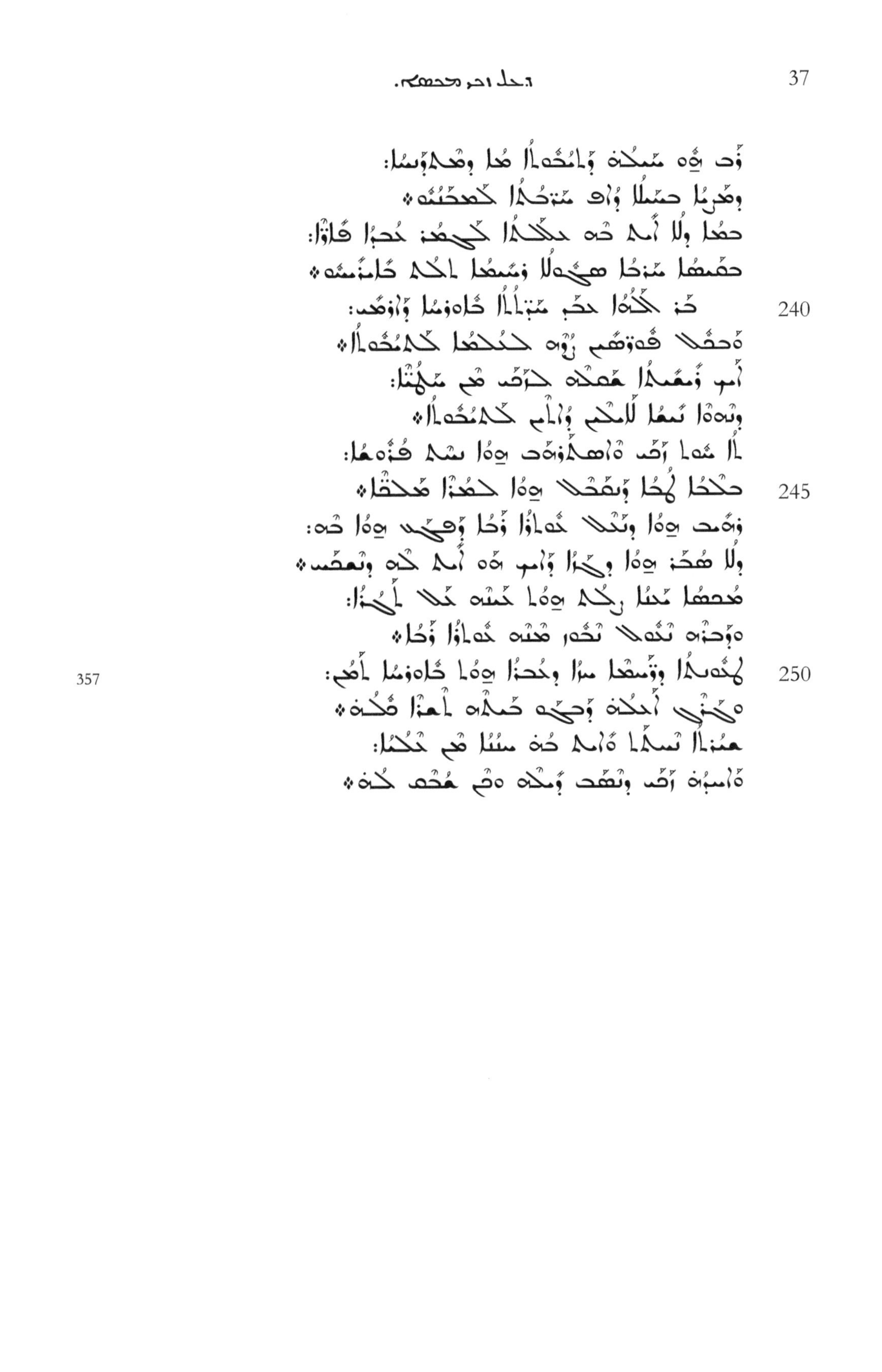

	Zacchaeus held it fast, releasing it only when he had taken what he desired.[35]
255	The chief tax-collector seized an encampment full of good things,
	one which from that hidden place[36] came down to terrestrial beings.
	With love he held that Merchant of mercy who had come,
	and he brought Him into his house to be enriched by His treasures. Lk 19:9
	O Zacchaeus, who robs both what is of earth and of Heaven,
260	who plunders both man and God and hides the spoils in his house!
	By you all the merchants on their ways were plundered;
	because of you the orphans, wronged in their accounts, cry out.
	Of you all the wayfarers complain in their inns,
	and against you even the inhabitants murmur when they take a day-long journey.
265	Mercy descended, walked upon earth, and you seized it;
	Loving Kindness journeyed from on high and you took it in.
	Grace had come, it was to traverse your region once again, and you laid hold of it;

---

[35] Lit. 'his own'.

[36] Hidden place, *atrâ gnizâ*: Bedjan gives a variant *atrâ ityâ*, hidden Being. *Atrâ* occurs frequently in the *Demonstrations* of Aphrahat. Golitzin analyzes these examples while giving the linguistic background: *maqom* in the Hebrew Bible as the place of divine manifestation, and *topos* in the LXX as "a stand in for God himself." In Rabbinic literature, particularly *hekhalot* texts, *maqom* is actually used as a divine name. See A. Golitzin, "The Place of the Presence of God." See also Golitzin, "Image and Glory of God," 338, 354–55. On *maqom* in Tannaitic sources see Urbach, *The Sages*, 66–79.

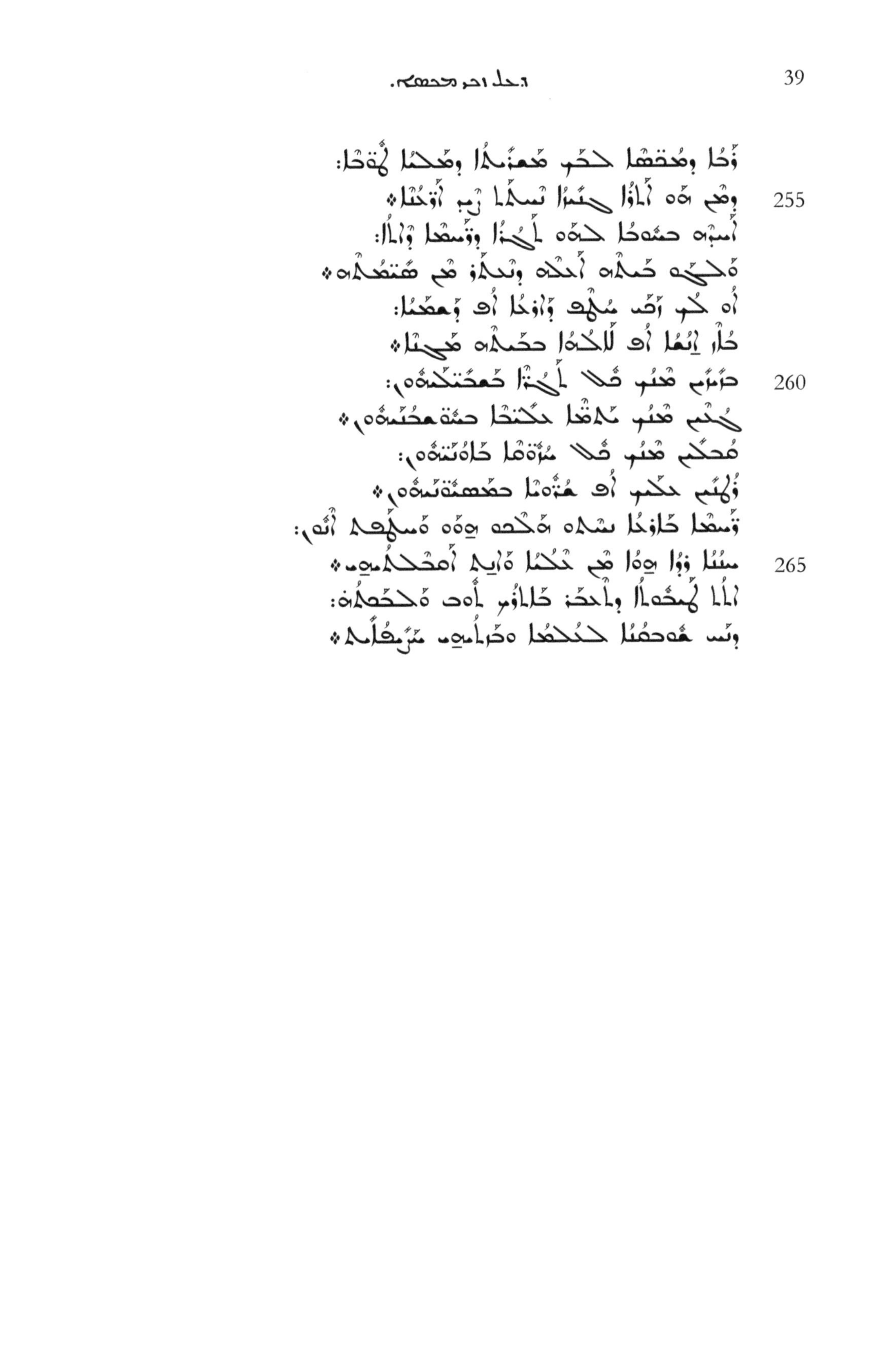

Forgiveness dawned upon the world, and you plundered it without shame.

The gift of peace came to earth, and see, it is in your house:
270   intrepidly you venture to gain possession of both Heaven and earth.

O Zacchaeus, you overwhelm me,[37] and how I shall speak of you I know not;

I marvel at you, O victorious one replete with victory.[38]

I should call you a tax-collector, but you are an apostle to the repentant;

you are also a disciple, O plunderer among the extortioners.

275   In everything you are the best, and I am too feeble to speak of you;

for tax-collectors you are a chief, and for the apostles a colleague and companion.

In the world you have your wealth, and in apostleship you are illustrious;

you suffer no poverty, and yet your fame is joined with the disciples.

You are secure in riches and assiduous in harvesting,
280   for you know how to seize, and it is not difficult for you to dispense.

Readily and easily you both amass and disperse;

you have the strength to cause wailing, to plunder, and to make yourself righteous.

On the one side your hand fills itself by seizure and robbery,

and on the other it lavishes upon all men alms of every kind.

285   In your way of life there is iniquity, and in your house the Son of God:

---

[37] A play on words in Syriac: *zkaytun zkkai*.
[38] A further play on Zacchaeus' name.

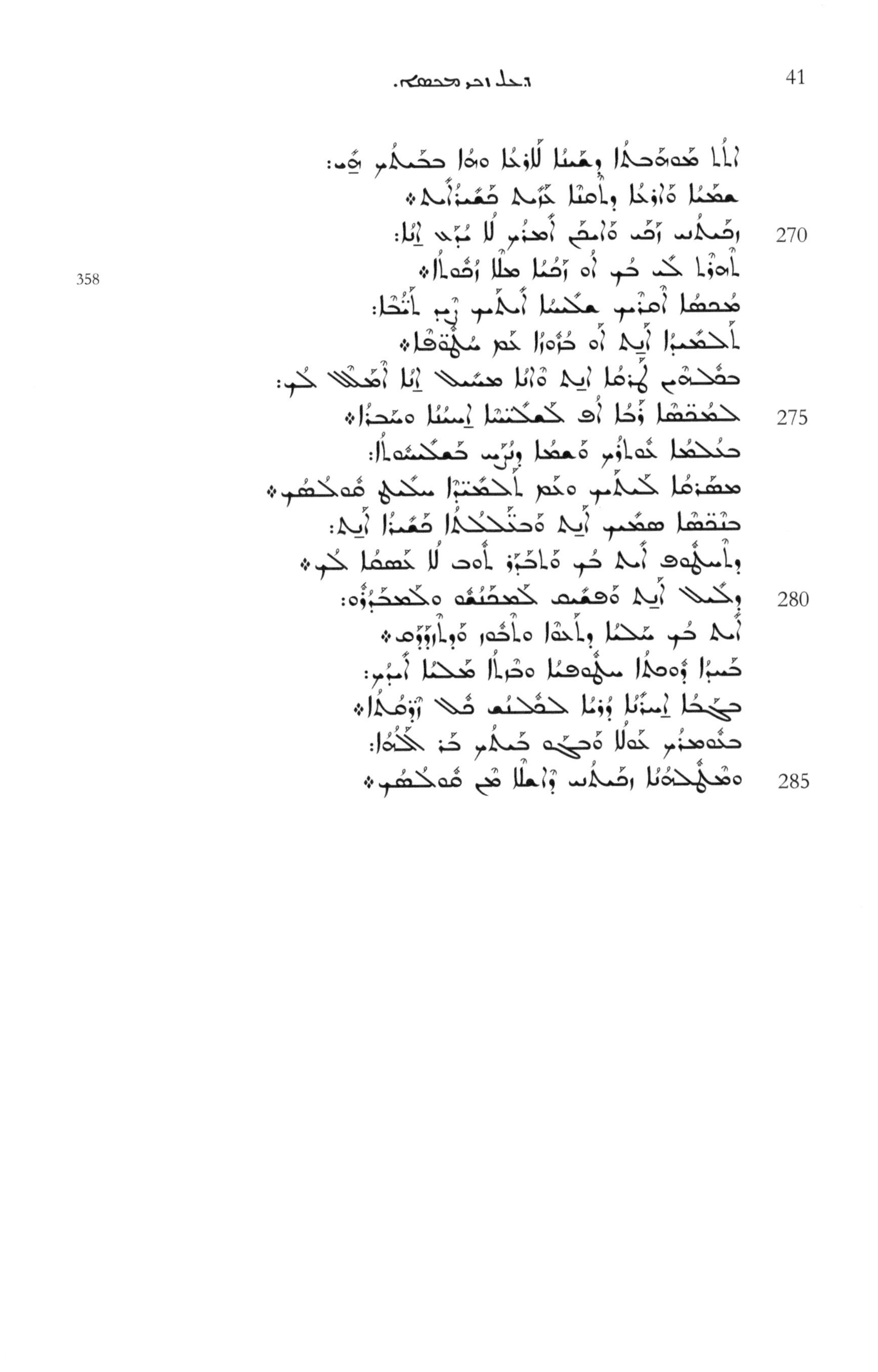

therefore you so overwhelm me that I must cease from your praise.

THE LORD OF THE WORLD RECLINES IN THE HOUSE OF ZACCHAEUS

The Son of God invited Himself to the home of Zacchaeus,   Lk 19:5
so as to give salvation to those who were in need of forgiveness.
The Physician came to the sick to drive out the sicknesses of iniquity,
290 but the blind multitudes bitterly reproached Him as He restored health.
"Why has He gone to the house of a tax-collector filled with evils?   Lk 19:7
Why does He keep company with sinners and show them love?   Lk 15:2
Why does He not turn away from association with the wicked, but He forgives them?
And why does He mingle with the lawless and favour them?
295 Why, if He is true, does He not despise the workers of iniquity?
For what reason does He eat with transgressors and they are dear to Him?"
The Shepherd was blamed as He sought out the lost sheep,   Lk 15:4-6
being very earnest in His quest, He ardently persisted.
And the Nurse[39] was being diligent in cleansing the ulcers of odious iniquity,
300 these men murmured against Him because He healed those suffering from wounds.
The Hope of the wicked and of sinners, who reclined at that banquet,
is He who forgives the debts of the repentant.

---

[39] Nurse (*yâṣopâ*): a term found infrequently in early Syriac literature for Christ as healer.

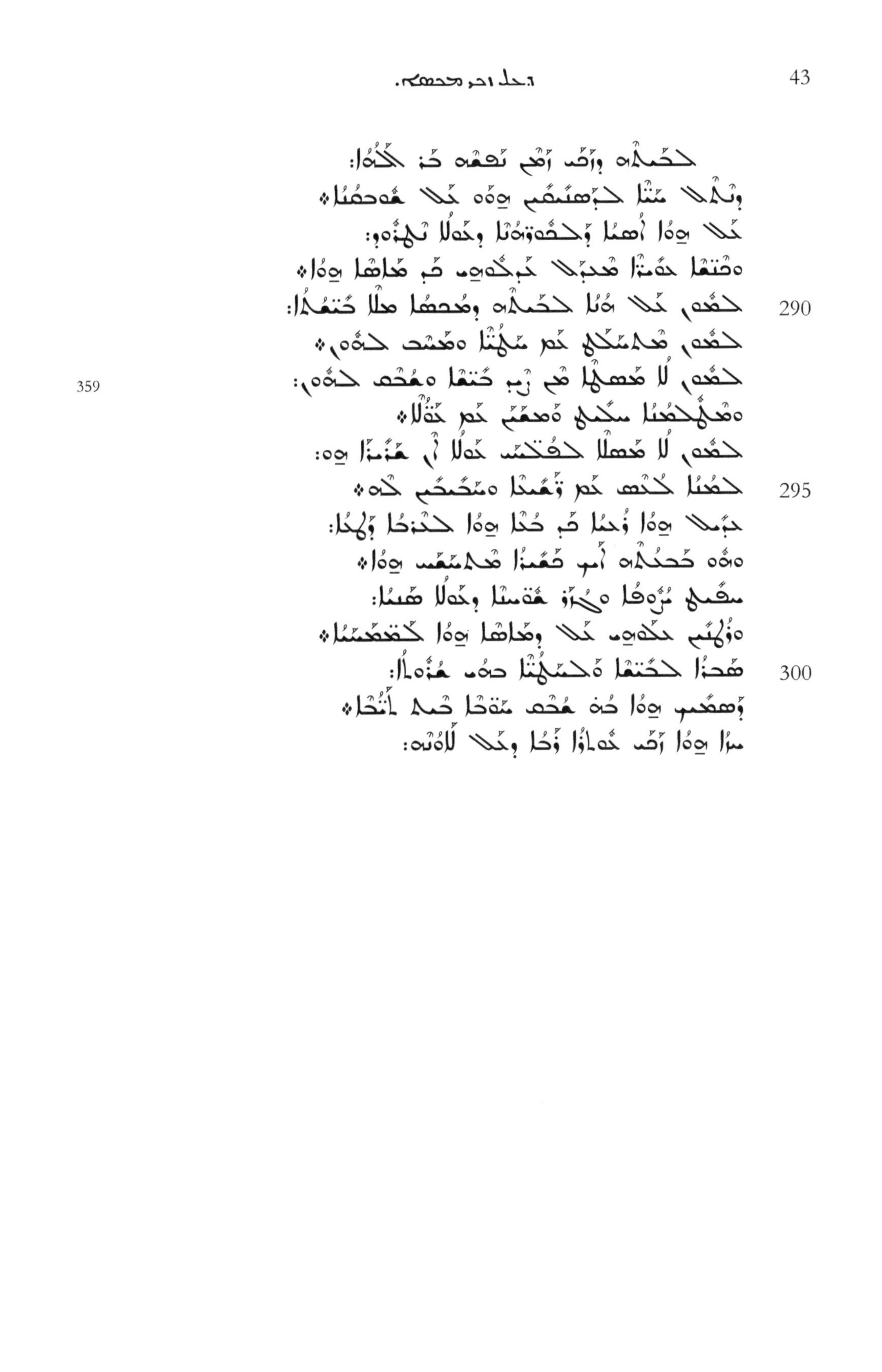

Zacchaeus saw the great wealth which had entered his lodging,   Lk 19:9
and he despised his goods so as to gain the treasure which he had found.
305   His soul was enlightened and he saw that the wealth of this world is iniquitous,
so he began to cast it from himself for the benefit of many.   Lk 19:8

He beheld the Lord of the world reclining at his feast,
and he despised the world and began to flee from its evils.

He, the prudent one, drew nigh and worshipped the Son, saying:
310   "I worship You, O Physician, who have visited me, stricken as I am with wounds.

A soul tormented by running sores will confess You, O Lord,
for when Your mercy has cleansed it, it will behold Your beauty clearly.

One stricken with many ulcers supplicates You,
for, as one solicitous, You did not find it loathsome to bind up my wounds.

315   My feeble mouth will give thanks to Your mouth which uttered sweet words
in my ears, that I might turn toward You and away from offences.

My lips will kiss Your feet, O Physician of many remedies,
for as soon as You visited me, my sickly members found relief.

I shall lick the dust of Your holy footprints,
320   for by Your steps You have driven out the iniquity which dwelt in me.

Let the half of my goods be a payment for the toil of Your feet, O Physician,
for though I am unworthy of Your visitation, You came to me.   Lk 1:43

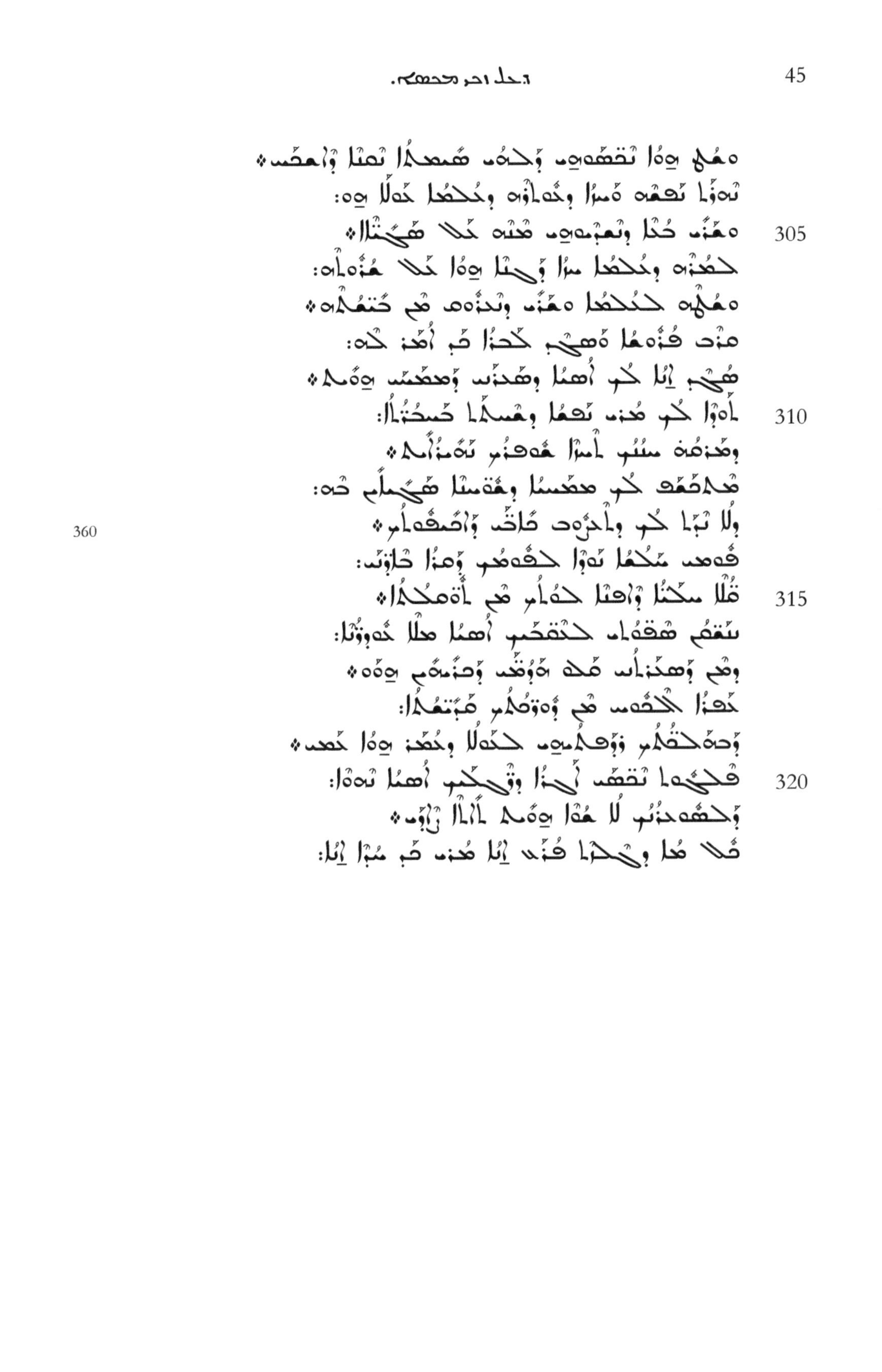

Whatsoever I have taken unjustly, O Lord, I restore with joy,
and the iniquity which I have done I shall change into righteousness.

325 That which I have appropriated through usury I shall return,
and whatsoever I have seized by force I shall restore twice over to the wronged.

Far be it that ever again I should usher iniquity within my gates,
or that baneful wickedness should be perpetrated within my mansion!

The door, whereby the great King entered to abide with me,
330 I shall not open again to sin to give it entry."

AT THE GREAT BANQUET, YOKED BY CHRIST, ZACCHAEUS BEGINS TO LAVISH HIS WEALTH UPON THE NEEDY

Christ wrought a great work at that feast,
for indeed, He did not hunger to eat bread without some motive.

A great banquet for repentance was held there
in the tax-collector's house, and He invited all sinners to it.

335 A wedding feast[40] was held wherein righteousness was exalted,   Mt 22:10, Jn 2:1, Rev 19:7,9
and our Lord went to make merry with the repentant.

---

[40] The image of wedding feast (*meštutâ*) in Jacob's theology takes in all salvation history. Here the banquet is being held in Zacchaeus's house to celebrate his repentance and the righteousness brought by Christ. The marriage feast in Eden was disrupted; Christ seeks to restore it in the Kingdom. His encounter with Zacchaeus is a sign which prepares for the eschatological banquet. See Ephrem's treatmernt of wedding imagery in Brock, *The Luminous Eye*, 115–41.

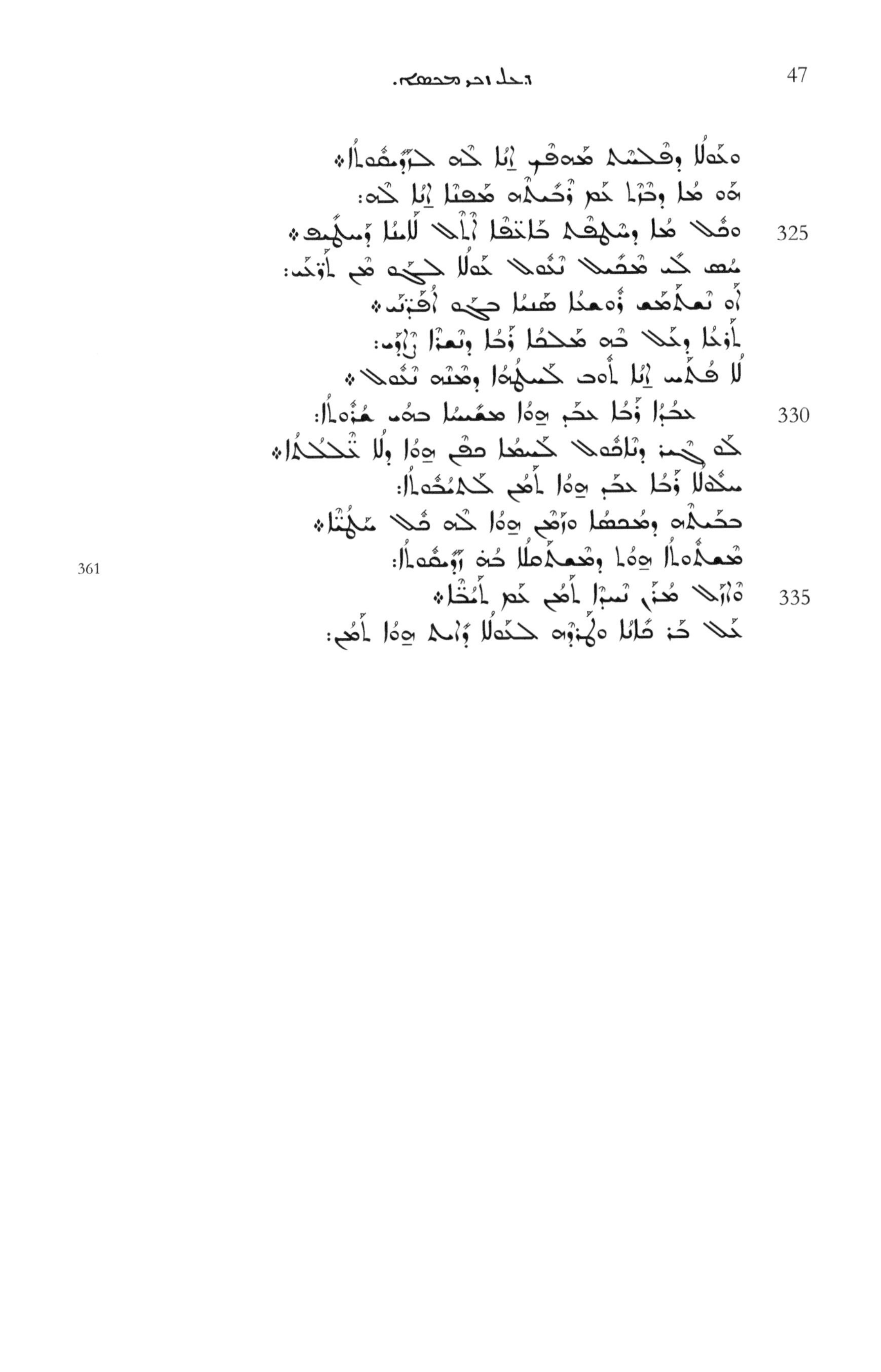

The Son of the Just One came and drove out the
    wickedness which resided there,
for darkness could not dwell together with the Re-
    splendent One.

Zacchaeus began to lavish his wealth upon the needy
340 and to disperse all his goods to those in distress.

He carried alms in his right hand and in his left,
and with both he diligently distributed them.

He was as quick to disperse as he was quick to amass,   Lk 19:8
for in every aspect in all that he encountered he was
    assiduous.

345 His doors are open, he fetches and sends forth again;
he raises his voice, calling all whom he had plundered
    to come and receive:

"You who have been robbed, come, receive back your
    own from the plunderer;
today is a day of retribution: let no one be reluctant to
    come to me!

Come, you poor, receive alms from a grasper;
350 you needy of the region, help me swiftly to disperse
    my wealth.

You who are in want, be labourers for me for a hand-
    some wage:
take in and remove this iniquity of mine which my
    debts[41] have so increased."

He was glad as he hastened to give out alms
and to distribute his wealth to all who came from
    every side.

355 The plunder, which had gradually flowed in as he re-
    joiced,
in one hour he brought forth and gave away, exulting.

He beheld the Son and his eyes were filled with His
    beauty,
and no longer could he gaze upon the world with
    love.

---

[41] 'Guilty debts'.

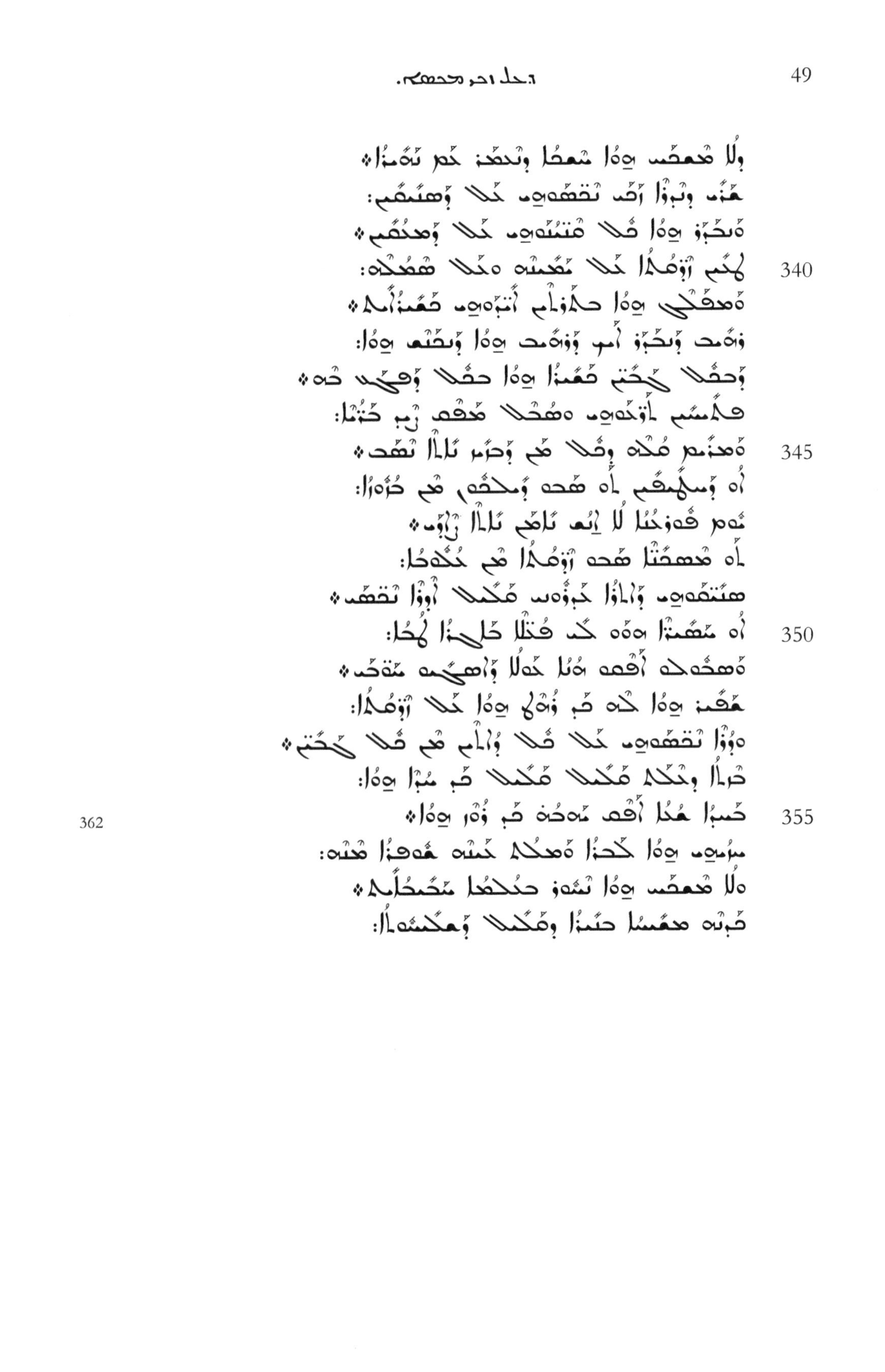

360	Christ yoked[42] him to the light yoke of apostleship in the manner that he had been pleased to bend his shoulder to riches.	Mt 11:29-30
	He willed to the Gospel one half of his goods when he encountered it, and he did not tarry to bring forth and give what he had promised.	Lk 19:8
	His hands carried righteousness to distribute, and his eyes were alert for the poor to receive them.	
365	His feet ran along the streets after passers-by to disperse his wealth with love to whomever was in need.	

A SOUL RESTORED FROM WICKEDNESS IS A GREATER SIGN THAN A BODY'S RESURRECTION FROM DESTRUCTION

This work, then, was transacted at that banquet,
but the foolish found fault, saying, "Why does He eat with sinners?"   Lk 15:2, Jn 11:38-44

Not so great a thing was it that He raised a dead man to life after corruption[43] had set in,

370 as it was that He made this chief of the tax-collectors an apostle.

Yes truly, it was a most awesome wonder,[44]
that a man so covetous should divide and give away all that he possessed.

Greater is it to restore a soul to life from out of much wickedness
than to raise up a body from perdition.

---

[42] Yoked (*kadneh*): Aphrahat speaks about the devotion of the yoked-one to his Lord and what this implies, see Koltun-Fromm, "Yokes of the Holy-Ones."

[43] Corruption (*da-sri*).

[44] Wonder (*tehrâ*) occurs several times in this homily and frequently throughout Jacob's writings. See his *mimro* "On the 'Wondrous' Name that Our Lord was called." Also in his *Letters* the term is frequently used. On the exegetical dimensions of *tehrâ* in Jacob and in other Syriac writers see my "Insight without Sight."

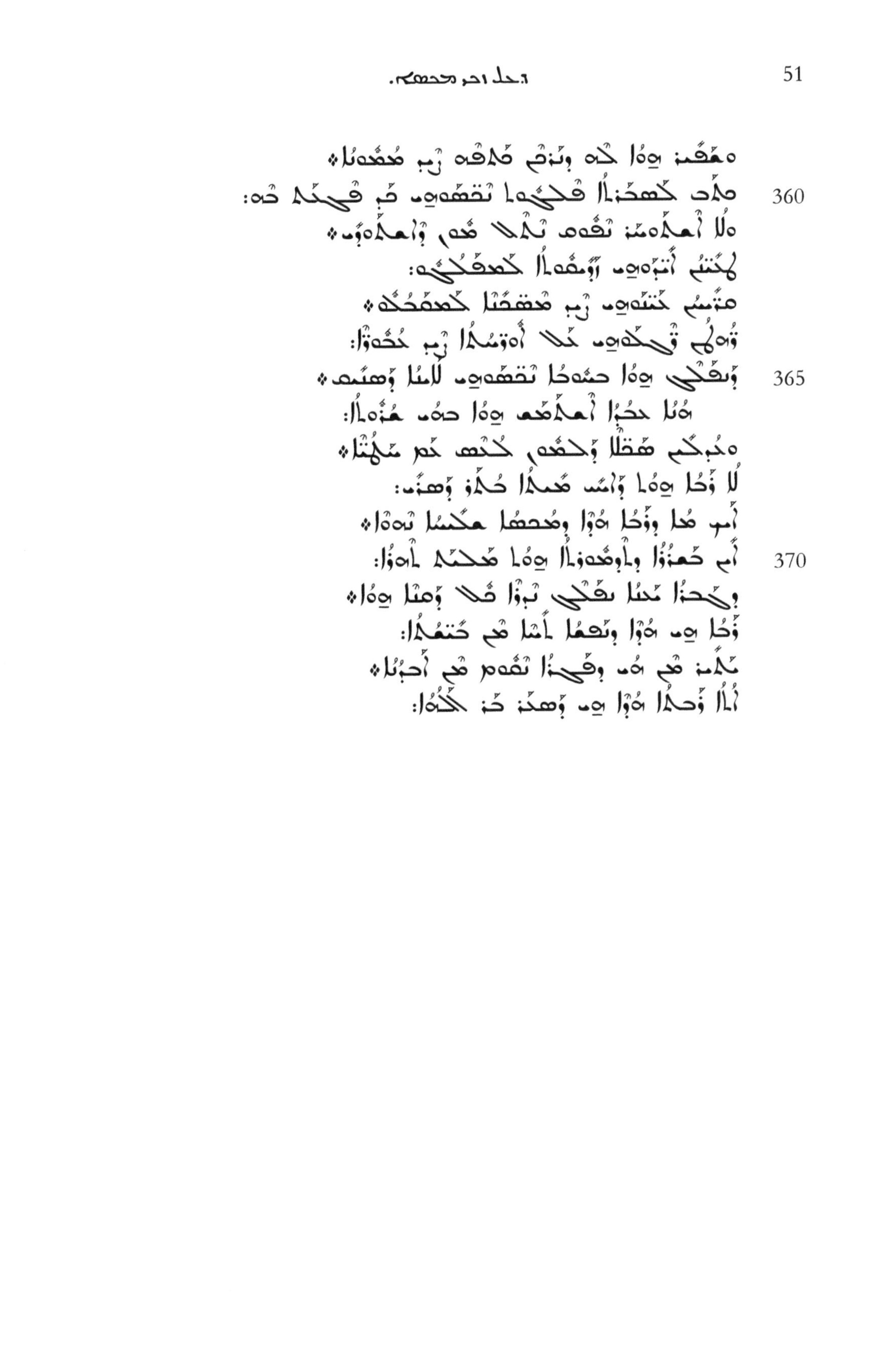

375	This is the great sign[45] that the Son of God wrought,
	when in a single moment He made a sinner into a righteous person.
	Where are the multitudes who found fault when He entered
	the house of the tax-collector to eat bread with sinners?
	They knew not how to view rightly what He was doing;
380	wise was the heart which used it for its own profit.
	That most sagacious Fisherman[46] cast His hook
	and caught by His mercies the ruler of the town.
	He enclosed the chief tax-collector in the net which He cast there,
	for indeed, no one ever fished thus save our Lord.
385	Into the sea of the world the Son of God cast His net, — Mt 13:47-8
	and it caught the tax-collector, dragging in with him his possessions as well.
	If our Lord had not gone into his home to eat bread, — Lk 19:5
	this catch would not have fallen into the net.
	If He had passed by and not invited Himself to come — Lk 19:5
	to the tax-collector,
390	this trove of repentance would not have been found.
	Indeed, He knew what He was doing where He tarried,
	and for this reason He was not concerned over the reproach.
	Our Lord saw Zacchaeus and rejoiced over the child He had gained,
	and began to call him a son of Abraham by reason of His love. — Lk19:9

---

[45] Sign (*âtâ*): see Bou Mansour, *Éphrem*, 57–61.

[46] Fisherman (*ṣayâdâ*): in the "Homily on Our Lord" Ephrem applies the term to Christ but elsewhere he uses it in reference to Apostles and to bishops. See Murray, *Symbols*, 176–78.

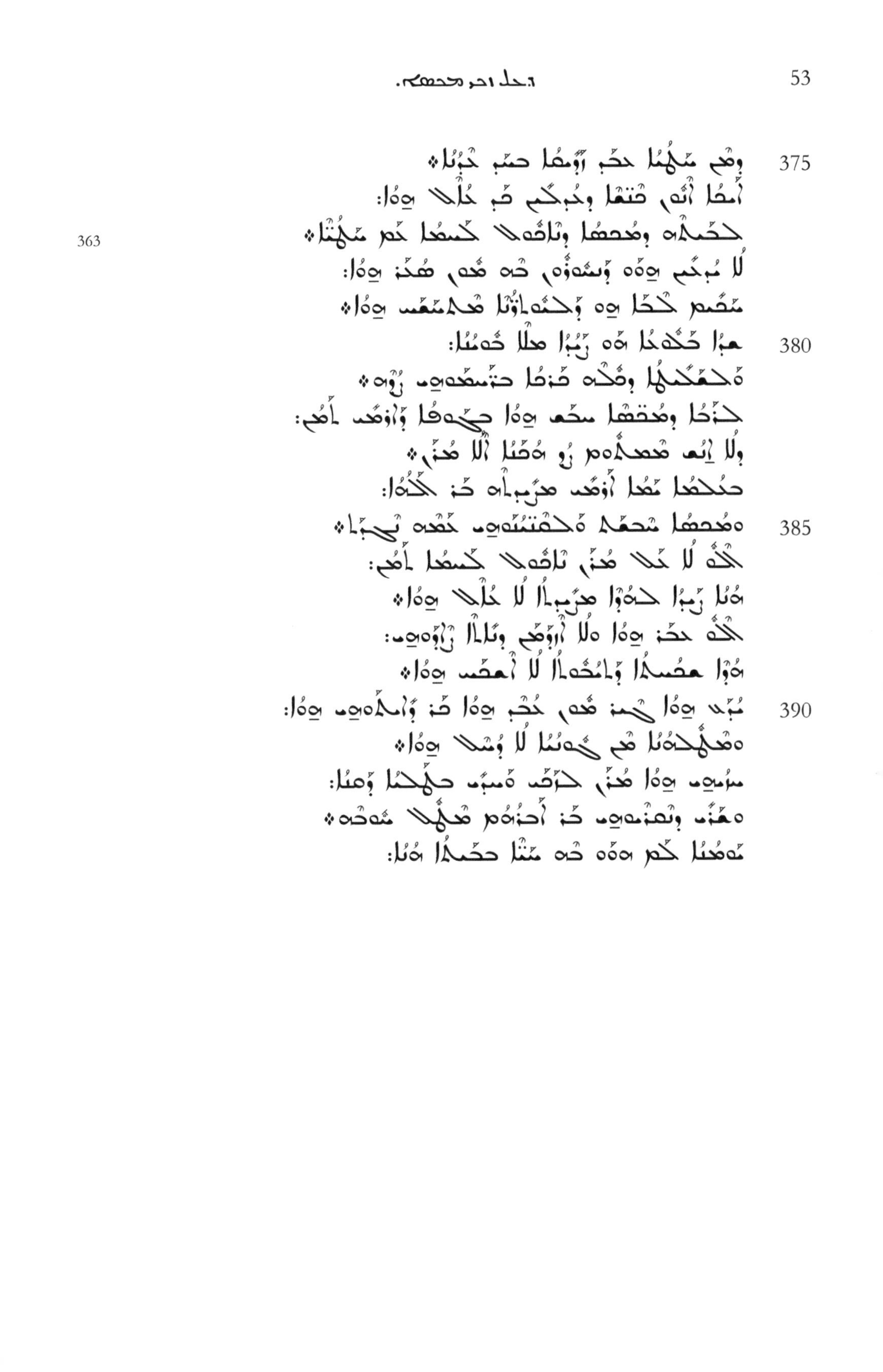

395 "Today", He said, "there is life in this house,
for life has dawned in it, and the death which reigned here has fled away."[47]
Behold, encouragement for all the wicked and for sinners,
that they too can become good through repentance!
Behold, the new deeds which the Son of God wrought on His path:
400 blessed is He who has proclaimed good hope to humanity.

---

[47] Life/ salvation: in early Syriac writings there is a sense of 'salvation' (Lk. 19:9, *sōtēria*; Peshitta, *ḥayē*) as being 'brought to life,' hence the interchangeability of the terms. For a discussion of what this implies see Klijn, "The Term Life," see also Lenzi, "The Syriac Usage of the Term Life."

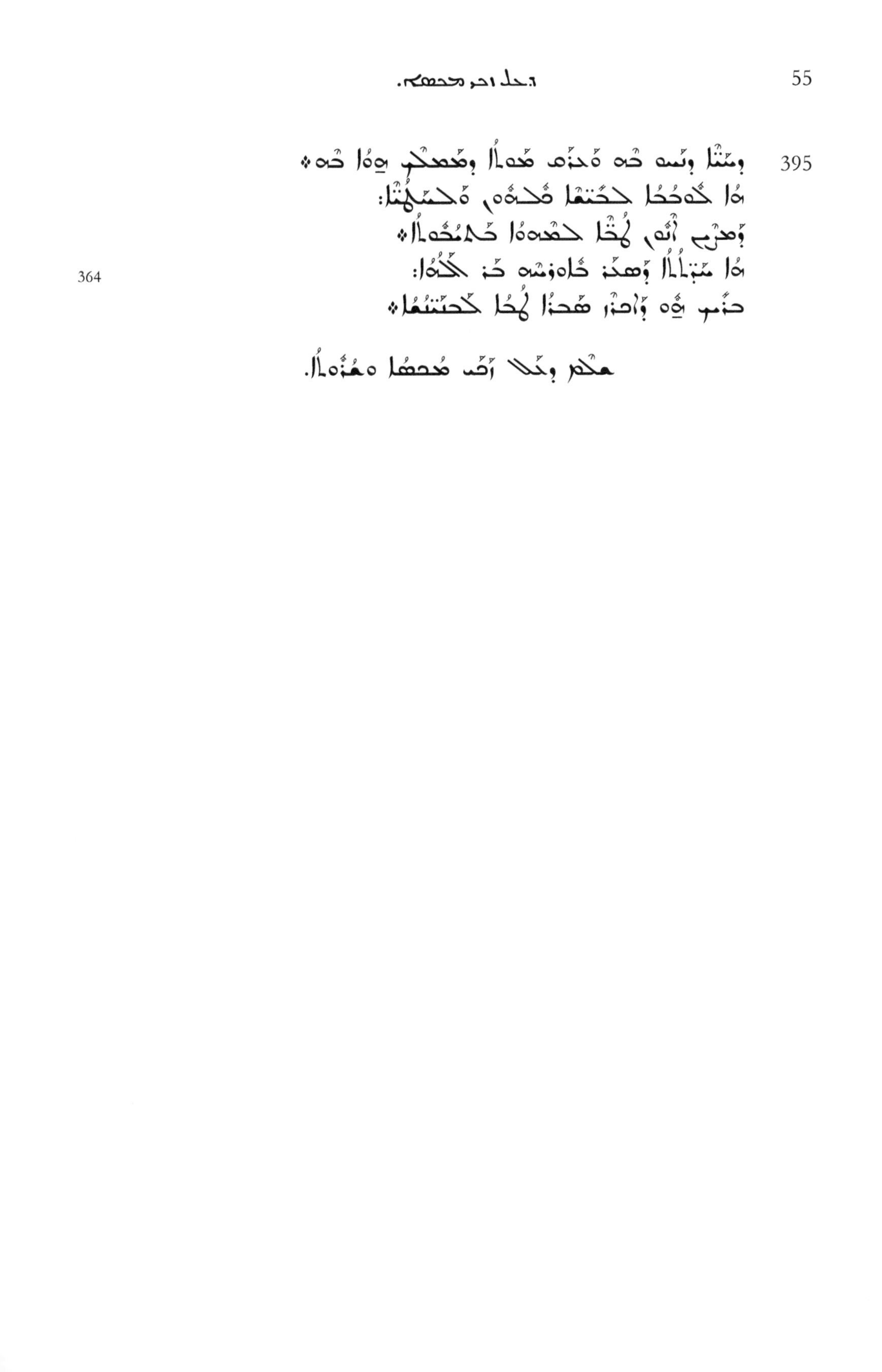

BIBLIOGRAPHY OF WORKS CITED

(A) ANCIENT AUTHORS AND TRANSLATIONS

Aphrahat:
K. Valavanolickal, *Demonstrations* I (Kerala,1999); II (Kottayam: SEERI, 2005).

Cyrillona:
C. Vona, *I Carmi di Cirillona* (Rome/Paris, 1963).

Ephrem:
S.P. Brock, "Ephrem's Letter to Publius," *LM* 89 (1976) 261–305.
S.P. Brock, *Hymns on Paradise* (Crestwood, 1990).
Commentaire de l'Évangile Concordant, Texte syriaque, ed. L. Leloir, Chester Beatty Monographs 8 (Dublin, 1963; French trans. L. Leloir, SC 121 [Paris, 1966]).
Homily "On Admonition and Repentance," Nicene and Post-Nicene Fathers, 2nd series vol. XIII, 330–36.
"Homily on Our Lord" in *St. Ephrem. Selected Prose Works* (Washington DC, 1994) 269–332.
C. McCarthy, *St. Ephrem's Commentary on Tatian's Diatessaron* (*JSS* Supplement 2, 1993).
K. McVey, "Hymns on Virginity" in *Ephrem the Syrian. Hymns* (New York, 1999).

Jacob:
M. Albert, *Les Lettres de Jacques de Saroug*, Patrimoine Syriaque-3 (Kaslik, 2004).
P. Bedjan, *Homiliae Selectae Mar-Jacobi Sarugensis*, I–V (Paris/Leipzig, 1905–1910; repr. Piscataway, 2006).
S.P. Brock, *Jacob of Serug's Homily on the Veil on Moses' Face* (Piscataway NJ, 2009).

S.F. Johnson, "The Sinful Woman: a memra by Jacob of Serug," *Sob/ECR* 24:1 (2002) 56–88.
E. Khalifé-Hachem, "Homélie Métrique de Jacques de Saroug sur l'Amour," *PdO* 1:2 (1970) 281–99
T. Kollamparampil, *Select Festal Homilies* (Bangalore, 1997).
J. Konat, "A metrical homily of Jacob of Serug on the mysteries, types and figures of Christ: authentic or compilation?," *LM* 118 (2005) 71–86.
G. Olinder, *Jacobi Sarugensis. Epistulae quotquot supersunt*, *CSCO* 110/syr 57 (Louvain, 1965).

Narsai:

J. Frishman, "Memra on the Brazen Serpent," *The Ways and Means of the Divine Economy* (diss. Leiden, 1992) http://public.me.com/ophirmm

Odes of Solomon:

J.H. Charlesworth, *The Odes of Solomon* (California, 1977).
J.A. Emerton, *The Odes of Solomon* in *The Apocryphal Old Testament* ed. H.F.D. Sparks (Oxford, 1984).

Rabbinics:

The Babylonian Talmud (London, 1938).
Midrash Rabbah (London, 1951).

Theodore of Mopsuestia:

R.C. Hill, *Theodore of Mopsuestia. Commentary on the Twelve Prophets* (Washington DC, 2003).

(B) MODERN WORKS

T. Bou Mansour, *La pensée symbolique de saint Ephrem* (Kaslik, 1988).
——, *La théologie de Jacques de Saroug*, I–II (Kaslik, 1993, 2000).
S.P. Brock, "Dieu Amour et Amour de Dieu chez Jacques de Saroug," *Patrimoine Syriaque* VIII, vol. 1 (Lebanon, 2003) 175–82.
——, "The Imagery of the Spiritual Mirror in Syriac Literature," *JCSSS* 5 (2005) 3–17.
——, *The Luminous Eye* (Kalamazoo MI, 1992).
J. Frishman, "Type and Reality in the Exegetical Homilies of Mar Narsai," *SP* 20 (1989) 169–75.

A. Golitzin, "The Image and Glory of God in Jacob of Serug's Homily, 'On that Chariot that Ezekiel the Prophet Saw'," *SVTQ* 47:3–4 (2003) 323–64.

——, "The Place of the Presence of God: Aphrahat of Persia's Portrait of the Christian Holy Man," 1–31.
http://www.marquette.edu/maqom/aimilianus

S.H. Griffith, "The Image of the Image Maker in the Poetry of St. Ephrem the Syrian," *SP* 25 (1993) 258–69.

M.T. Hansbury, "'Insight without Sight': Wonder as an Aspect of Revelation in the Discourses of Isaac the Syrian," *JCSSS* 8 (2008) 60–73.

S. Harvey, "Embodiment in Time and Eternity: a Syriac Perspective," *SVTQ* 43.2 (1999)105–30.

——, "St. Ephrem on the Scent of Salvation," *JTS* NS, 49.1 (1998), 109–28.

A.F.J. Klijn, "The Term Life in Syriac Theology," *SJT* 9(1962) 390–7.

T. Kollamparampil, *Salvation according to Jacob of Serugh* (Bangalore, 2001).

N. Koltun-Fromm, "Yokes of the Holy-Ones: The Embodiment of a Christian Vocation," *HTR* 94.2 (2001) 205–218.

J. Konat, "Christological Insights in Jacob of Serug's Typology as Reflected in His *Memre*," *ETL* 77(2001) 46–72.

G. Lenzi, "The Syriac Usage of the Term 'Life' for "Salvation" Reconsidered," *JNSL* 32/1 (2006) 83–95.

R. Murray, *Symbols of Church and Kingdom. A Study in Early Syriac Tradition* (Cambridge,1975; revised ed. Piscataway, NJ, 2004).

J. Neusner, *Symbol and Theology in Early Judaism* (Minneapolis MN,1991).

F. Rilliet, "La Louange des Pierres," *RTP* 117 (1985) 293–304.

——, "La métaphore du chemin dans la sotériologie de Jacques de Saroug," *SP* 25 (1993) 324–31.

A. Shemunkasho, *Healing in the Theology of Saint Ephrem* (Piscataway NJ, 2002).

C. Stewart, *'Working the Earth of the Heart,' The Messalian Controversy in History, Texts and Language to AD 431* (Oxford, 1991).

E. Urbach, *The Sages* (Jerusalem, 1979).

INDEX OF NAMES AND THEMES

Abraham 394
Adam 113, 227, 230
apostle, apostleship 42, 54, 187, 212, 273, 276, 277, 359, 370
bread 215, 332, 387
Christ, titles of
    Doctor 28
    Fisherman 381
    Fruit of Life 120
    Herb of Life 78
    Hope 301
    Husbandman 207
    Judge 81
    Just One 79
    King 329
    Lofty One 138
    Lord of Eden 116
    Lord of kings 246
    Lord of the world 307
    Merchant 249
    Merchant of mercy 257
    Nurse 299
    Physician 11, 34, 50, 75, 94, 289, 310, 317, 321
    Resplendent One 338
    Saviour 33, 172, 177
    Shepherd 47, 200, 297
    Son of God 53, 132, 241, 285, 287, 375, 385, 399
    Son of the Just One 337
    Sweet Fruit 180
cluster 240

corruption 369
Creator 230
desire 155, 157, 159-160, 161, 163, 165, 168, 170
destruction 32
disciple 274, 278
Eden 225
faith 129, 135
fashioned anew 151
first fruit 211, 223, 243
forgiveness 14, 24, 188, 268, 288
formations 106
fruit 213, 218, 221, 223, 225, 234, 239
grace 83, 267
harlot 7, 9, 65, 211
health, healing 22, 76, 290, 300
Hebrews 146
hope 192, 400
bronze serpent 147
hidden serpent 143
image 195
iniquity, wickedness 26, 29, 62, 64, 65, 71, 75, 159, 289, 295, 299, 305, 320, 324, 327-328, 337, 373
Jericho 226, 233, 240
joined 162-68
joy 323
Judea 73
justice 38
life/salvation 192, 288, 395-396
lodge, abide 205, 329

lost sheep 87, 200, 297
love 10, 23, 74, 98, 100, 102, 131, 154-56, 161-64, 169-72, 174, 175, 182, 185, 206, 231, 257, 292, 358, 366, 394
lowliness 138
marvel, wonder, admire 53, 196, 272, 371
medicine 17, 21, 25
mercy, compassion 30, 32, 188, 194, 197, 251, 253, 265, 312, 382
mingle 51, 162-68, 294
mirror 39
pattern 244
path, way 1, 3, 241, 399
peace 269
place 117, 256

portray 195
repentance 35, 45, 85, 195, 231, 237, 239, 242, 244, 333, 390, 398
resurrection 13
righteousness 153, 324, 335, 363, 141
sign 375
stones, rocks 213-214
sweet fruit 210, 220
sweet savour 224
fig tree, passim
truth 160
wedding feast 335
wine 215
yoke 359
Zacchaeus, passim

INDEX OF BIBLICAL REFERENCES

Genesis
  3:7 — 113
  3:7–8 — 227-28
  3:10 — 230
Exodus
  3:7 — 216
  16:31 — 215
  17:5-6 — 214
Numbers
  21:6 — 143-50
  21:9 — 144, 146, 147
  21:4–9 — 150
Deuteronomy
  8:16 — 215
Psalms
  25:8 — 3
  34:18 — 19
  51:13 — 3
  51:17 — 19
  109:22 — 20
  147:3 — 19
Isaiah
  61:1 — 20
Hosea
  6:1 — 11
  9.10 — 211, 223, 243
Jeremiah
  33:6 — 11
Matthew
  9:12 — 11
  9:9 — 212
  11:19 — 9
  11:29–31 — 359
  13:47-8 — 385-6
  15:24 — 5, 200
  15:32–7 — 216
  17:24–7 — 219
  22:1–10 — 335
  22:15–22 — 217
  27:51–3 — 213
Mark
  2:17 — 11
Luke
  1:43 — 322
  5:29–31 — 9
  5:31 — 11
  7:34 — 9
  7:38 — 7
  7:41–3 — 23-4
  10:34 — 10
  15:1 — 9
  15:2 — 4, 292, 368
  15:4 — 5, 200
  15:4–6 — 200, 297
  15:24 — 200
  19:5 — 201, 287, 387, 389
  19:7 — 291
  19:8 — 306, 343, 361
  19:9 — 258, 303, 394, 396
  19:10 — 5, 200
  19:40 — 213
John
  2:1 — 335
  2:1–11 — 215
  3:14 — 147

8:28	147	I Timothy	
10:11	200	1:15	3
11:38-44	368	James	
12:32	147	1:18	211, 223, 243
		Revelation	
I Corinthians		14:4	211, 223, 243
10:4	214	19:7, 9	335